FLORINE L

MOJAVE DESERT TRAILS

BY THE AUTHOR OF **OUT FROM LAS VEGAS**

SPOTTED DOG PRESS.

BISHOP ❧ CALIFORNIA

Headworks and ruins at Atolia PHOTO: WYNNE BENTI

FLORINE LAWLOR

MOJAVE DESERT TRAILS

BY THE AUTHOR OF **OUT FROM LAS VEGAS**

PHOTOGRAPHS BY LESLIE PAYNE AND WYNNE BENTI

SPOTTED DOG PRESS®

BISHOP 🐾 CALIFORNIA

Mojave Desert Trails
©1989-2004 Florine Lawlor

SPOTTED DOG PRESS®

ISBN Number: 1-893343-03-0
Spotted Dog Press, Inc.
Box 1721, Bishop, CA 93515-1721
**Order online at www. SpottedDogPress.com
or call TOLL-FREE 800-417-2790**

Library of Congress Cataloging-in-Publication Data

Lawlor, Florine
    Mojave Desert Trails / Florine Lawlor.
    p. cm.
    Includes bibliographical references and index.
    ISBN 1-893343-03-0 (alk. paper)
        1. Historic sites--California--Mojave Desert. 2. Trails--California--Mojave Desert. 3. Mojave Desert (Calif.)--History, Local. 4. Historic sites--California--Mojave Desert--Guidebooks.
        5. Trails--California--Mojave Desert--Guidebooks. 6. Mojave Desert (Calif.)--Guidebooks. I. Title.
        F868.M65L395 2004
        979.4'95--dc22
                                                            2004045219

Printed in the United States of America

Table of Contents

PREFACE
FLORINE LAWLOR

San Bernardino County is a treasure trove of secret places waiting to be explored—dark winding canyons, lofty mountain peaks, deep washes, and ghost towns—all remnants of the Old West's colorful past. And what a past it was, from the dawn of the planet's creation when volcanic upheavals formed Cima Dome, Amboy Crater and what is now the Cinder Cone National Natural Landmark, a valley of thirty-two volcanic cones south of Baker and Mitchell Caverns to more recent times when prehistoric artists, ancient ancestors of the Mohaves, Chemehuevis, Paiutes and Shoshone left their marks on the hard rock fascia of lava flows. Thousands of years passed before the Spanish came, followed by settlers of European descent—over the Spanish Trail and the Old Government Road, leaving settlements and camps, an Army outpost at Camp Cady and the redoubts of Marl Springs. Prospectors and miners left their marks on the land and mountains, with mine shafts and yawning glory holes. Some went out with pockets full of gold, while many others lost everything. Even their lives.

Today the county of San Bernardino boasts territory in the Mojave Desert that remains comparatively untouched, in sharp contrast the sprawling cities of Southern California that border the region. The outlying area of San Bernardino County is a hermit kingdom, with salty dry lakes, tall swaying conifers and more stories than a single volume on this expanse of desert can hope to record.

The trips in this book are but a few of my favorite places. The maps and directions are as accurate as we could make them, but roads do change with each rainfall and/or windstorm, so sometimes yesterday's trail is completely obliterated by tomorrow. But with patience and persistence, you will find many of them.

All trips in this guide are made over paved roads, county graded roads, or routes which have stood the passage of time in their usage, such as old mining tracks, some dating as far back as the Old Government Road. There are no "outlaw" cross-country routes. Hence, we cannot call this a book of "jeep trails" so, it is a guide to the desert trails of the Mojave.

FOREWORD
WALT WHEELOCK

The prehistory of the Mojave Desert concerned perhaps four tribes: Southern Paiutes and Chemehuevis, early, commonly referred to as "Pah-Utes," the Mohaves, (MOJAVE = California Place Names; MOHAVE = Indians and Arizona Names). Living primarily as "hunters and gatherers" the Chemehuevis and Southern Paiute lived inland near desert springs, growing vegetables on a very small scale.

The Mohaves and Yumas lived along the Colorado River. Each group was large and powerful, often fighting with their neighbors. These people traveled extensively, sometimes as far away as the shores of the Pacific Ocean.

While majority of desert Native Americans used a network of trails throughout the desert, the Mohaves mainly took two routes, to join the villages on the Colorado and an outlying camp at the Sink of the Mojave (Soda Lake). One of these from Fort Mohave went west via Rock Springs, Marl Spring, Rocky Ridge, Jackass Canyon and Soda Springs. It later became the wagon route known as the "Mojave Road." The other route, sometimes referred to as the "Pah-Ute Route" ran south of the Mojave Road (once called the Government Road) passing through Foshay Pass and north of the Kelso Dunes, finally picking up the Mojave River west of Soda Lake.

Early explorations into the deserts of California were quite rare. At first these were made by ships. Probably the first was that of Francisco de Ulloa, who sailed along the coasts of

Sinaloa and Sonora in 1539. The smallest ship was lost at sea, but the other two reached the mouth of the Colorado proving, contrary to the widely held belief, that California was not an island. They sailed south along the east coast of Baja California. Rounding the Cape, they continued north along the western shores to Cedros Island. From here one ship was sent home with the reports of the journey, while Ulloa sailed on. For how long he sailed and to where is unknown as records of the voyage were apparently lost.

In 1540 Hernando de Alarcon duplicated Ulloa's voyage up the west coast of Sonora to the mouth of the Colorado. His assignment was to find Coronado's grand (and struggling) expedition and supply them with provisions. Finding no trace of Coronado, he and his men continued up the Colorado in small boats, probably as far as the Gila River, before returning to his home port. He left notes below two different trees along the river bank, in case some of Coronado's men passed by.

Coronado had been gathering men, Indian scouts and porters as well as live stock in Nayarit. He moved north to Culiacan in April, 1540. His small entourage was well supplied with captains (six listed) as well as several caballeros (gentlemen, knights) who later became captains. Among the original six was "Melchior Diaz, a former alcade mayor and captain of Culiacan, who, although he was not a gentleman, deserved the appointment he held." Indeed, he was one of Coronado's most valuable aides.

Fray Marcos de Niza, a Franciscan priest, offered to take Esteban, a slave of African descent, to scout ahead to check Vaca's fabulous reports of golden cities and riches. Esteban had crossed the continent with Cabeza de Vaca. Niza's reports appeared to be to wild to be believable and Diaz was delegated to verify the reports.

Coronado assembled his small army in Culiacan. After spending two weeks there, the party went north, and established another camp on the Sonora River near the present town of Ures. Vaca had named this place Corazones. Wanting to find out if Alarcon had reached this point, Don Rodrigo Maldonado followed the Rio Sonora to the coast in search of a harbor with hopes of finding the ships. Though he did not find them, he talked with Seri Indians who reported seeing white-sailed vessels offshore. Maldonado returned and brought with him a Seri so tall that the biggest man in the army did not come up to his nipples.

During October, Captain Diaz returned from Cibola. He was to remain in the new town of Corazones, as captain in charge, with the goal of finding Alarcon and his ships.

After the army left for Cibola, Diaz was instructed to take half the men and explore the west. He took selected twenty-five men and set off with Native guides for the coast. Traveling 150 leagues they came to the river entered by Alarcon.

Many historians, including Bolton, believe that Diaz went north near the town of Magdalena, then west over the Camino del Diablo following the same route Anza would later use to reach Yuma.

It seems unlikely that Diaz would have traveled some 150 miles to the north, always moving away from the coast, before turning to the west. By the time of Anza's trek, Kino and Garces each had traveled this route on which a string of missions had been established as far west as Sonoyta. One report even claims that Diaz had traded corn for fish with the Indians on this route—most unlikely, if he had been some sixty miles from the seashore!

Many believe that the area between Kino Bay and the Colorado River delta was so arid that such a trip would have been impossible. The local Seris scoff at this, noting that their ancestors often made this very same trip, long before the coming of automobiles.

Castaneda's history merely states: After traveling some 150 leagues Diaz came to a province inhabited by people like giants, exceedingly tall and muscular... the captain learned through an interpreter that the ships of Alarcon had come up the river from the sea to a point within three days travel.

Diaz traveled to the spot and found the following written on a tree: "Alarcon came this far; there are letters at the foot of the tree." They learned how long Alarcon had waited for news of the army, before returning to New Spain.

Returning up river to a possible crossing Diaz began to worry about the Yuma Indians. He "questioned" a captive and discovered that the Yuma planned to attack in the morning, when the Spaniards were divided into three groups: east bank west bank and midstream. Tying a heavy rock onto the poor Indian, he was tossed into the stream to prevent him from warning the Yumas.

The next day, the Yumas came for war, showering arrows down on the Spaniards. Spanish horsemen overtook them, mercilessly cutting them down, while the musketeers took good aim The Yumas abandoned the field and took to the hills. All of Diaz' men were able to cross safely.

After they crossed the river, all went ahead in search of the coast. Melchior Diaz continued for five or six days to the west, but turned back because he did not find water or grass, only relentless sand dunes. They also encountered beds of burning lava, before turning back. During his return Melchior accidentally died while hurling a lance at a dog chasing sheep. The lance stuck upright in the ground while Diaz overran it, fatally piercing his spleen.

The story goes that Diaz had turned south to the hot springs near Cerro Prieto where there would have plenty of water. It is more reasonable to assume that he had continued west along the Yuma Dunes to the Mud Volcanos of the Salton Sink. Obsidian Butte, the only supply of obsidian in Southern California was close by. Indian trails converged at Obsidian Butte from all directions. After all, it was the source of material for arrowheads.

Two years later in 1542, Rodriguez Cabrillo, was sent to explore the Pacific coast of the California. En route, he received reports of the Yuma massacre by Spanish horsemen. From San Quintin to Santa Barbara, news traveled fast even in the sixteenth century

The first expedition to actually reach the Mojave Desert was that of Juan de Onate in 1604. A governor of New Mexico, he led an expedition to reach the "Mar del Sur" from that province. On October 7th, he headed west, visiting the Zunis and the Hopis before reaching the Little Colorado which he followed to the Bill Williams Fork. He traveled along the Bill Williams Fork to its junction with the Colorado, land of the Mohaves. They traveled down stream to the confluence with the Gila River inhabited by a large and "somewhat ruder people"—the Yuma Indians. Onate continued to the mouth of the Colorado, which he referred to as a fine harbor. The explorers then began the return journey, along the same route to New Mexico. Hence the Mohaves were twice visited by a Spanish army.

The first recorded trip from California to the Colorado River was made by a Baja California Cochimi Indian, Sebastian Tarabal. He had first traveled north from Mission Santa Gertrudis in 1769 with Portola and Serra. He returned to his home, on a trip with Rivera y Moncada in January, 1770. Then three years later, Father Palou, after turning over the Baja missions to the Dominicans, brought several Indians north with him. Sebastian and his wife Dolores were assigned to Mission San Gabriel. However, that mission was suffering from a severe food shortage, so, Sebastian, Dolores, and an unnamed male acquaintance went east into the desert, destination Colorado. They crossed over the San Jacinto range, into Anza-Borrego stopping at an Indian camp on the San Felipe Wash. Anza was later to name this "Cienega San Sebastian." Later reports of Sebastian's route east note that both Dolores and their friend died while all three crossed the Yuma sand dunes. This is an unfounded supposition. It seems highly unlikely that Sebastian would have attempted to cross the sand dunes. More likely, he would have traveled down the San Felipe Wash to the dry Salton Sink, then crossed on an Indian trail to Obsidian Butte. From here a wide level valley leads directly to Yuma crossing, the same route that Melchior Diaz may have taken two centuries earlier. Here he met a Yuma chief, whom he named "Salvador Palma" This chief promptly took him to the El Altar Presido, possibly hoping for a reward for turning in a runaway California Indian. Captain Anza, assembling his troops at Tubac, heard of Sebastian's arrival, and summoned him to act as his guide. Father Garces, who was Anza's guide, was not too happy with the appointment of Sebastian. When they reached Yuma, Garces took over. He led Anza south into Baja, but could not find a way west. Anza reports that "Sebastian was confused," which he would have been, as he had crossed north of the dunes. When the party finally reached the western end of the dunes, Sebastian pointed to the northern mountains undoubtedly calling out "Derecho!" Anza then traveled directly north to Cienega San Sebastian, where Sebastian was welcomed by his friends. From here it was an easy journey to Mission San Gabriel.

On Oct. 15, 1774, Anza again left Tubac, to convoy settlers north to what is now San Francisco. Father Garces and Sebastian were along, but left the expedition at the Yuma Crossing. The two explored south into Baja, and on February 14 started up the Colorado with three Mohave guides. Father Garces hoped to be able to locate a more direct route from Santa Fe to Monterey than the southern loop used by Anza.

Leaving the Mohave villages, he struck directly west on what the Mohaves called the "Pah-Ute Route," which ran south of the Mojave Road through Foshay Pass, then north of the Kelso Dunes to the Mojave River bed near Soda Lake. From here, his route passed the San Bernardino Mountains, and down to the San Gabriel Mission. Leaving the mission, Garces and Sebastian then crossed the San Gabriel Mountains into San Joaquin Valley. He attempted to find another route to Monterey, but failed.

He returned east, taking a more northerly route back to the Mojave villages. He planned on finding a direct route to Santa Fe. Sebastian was tired of the traveling. Garces told him to go down to the land of the Jacheduns (midway between the Mohaves and the Yumas). Months later, Garces reached the Hopi pueblo of Oraibi on the Colorado Plateau in what is now Arizona. The Hopi told him that it would not be safe to cross Apache land, so he returned to the Colorado River. From Yuma, he traveled east to Tubatama to write his report.

Following the discovery of gold in California and the thousands of settlers that came west, there was a strong demand for the construction of a transcontinental railroad. Bitter conflicts arose over the choice of a route. Congress authorized Secretary of War, Jefferson Davis to select routes and put engineers into the field. Four routes were chosen: (1) Northern, between the 47th and 49th parallels; (2) the Central or Benton route between the 38th and 39th; the Albuquerque on the 35th; and the extreme Southern on the 32nd parallel.

1854: Mojave Indians as drawn by Henrich Baldwin Molhausen
from the U.S. P. R. R. Exploration & Surveys, 35th Parallel (Volume III)
Whipple Railraod Survey Party lead by Lieutenant A.W. Whipple

None of these routes were ever used, however the railroad surveys of 1853 revealed the geography of the West, making valuable pathways to the Pacific Ocean known. Twelve volumes of the PACIFIC RAILROAD SURVEYS were published which not only covered the findings of a normal survey, but included geology, botany, animals and insects. At times, lengthy sections described the local Native Americans; their way of life, villages, tribes, agricultural methods, and feuds with neighbors.

Volume III, "Mississippi River to the Pacific Ocean," written by Lieutenant Amiel Weeks Whipple, contains a Chapter XV, "From the Colorado River to the Mormon Road," which describes in detail the route from what was to become Fort Mohave to the Soda Sink. This covers the core of the Mojave Desert. The proceeding chapter has an excellent report on the "Valley of the Mohaves" and the people that lived there. A brief report in Chapter XVI carries us to El Cajon Pass. In addition the volume contains a series of excellent full-page illustrations of the Mohaves.

Whipple arrived in the "Mohave Valley" on February 23, 1853. A lengthy survey was made of the valley, its fields, crops and villages. The party remained there until March 2nd, exploring the valley, bargaining trade goods for grain and other foodstuffs, and preparing for a river crossing. Whipple reported: "'The Indians were shrewd and would part with no articles without a really valuable compensation!"

The Mohaves offered to ferry the party across the Colorado, however Whipple had brought along an Indian rubber pontoon and this offer was declined. On the second crossing, in midstream the pontoon upset, throwing everything (and everyone) into the river. An enormous amount of time was spent trying to dry out gear, and save what was eventually ruined or lost. Many survey instruments were ruined, books and papers destroyed. Fortunately none of the field-notes or collections had been injured or lost.

Leaving on March 2, following an old foot path, almost due west, they made a dry camp that night. The next day they reached water and good grass at Pah-Ute Creek, and set up camp. (This and many of the following, place names were bestowed by Whipple.) On March 4, they continued on an Indian trail, reported to lead to Los Angeles, but again were forced to make a dry camp.

The next morning forty mules were missing, but finally located. Seven miles west a small spring was located. A basin was dug, and filled with enough water to supply the animals. This was given the name of "Rock Spring."

The next trip led again to a good campsite, eventually named "Marl Spring," where grazing was excellent. From here the next leg was thirty miles, as measured by their odometer. Their animals made the trip without trouble. They entered dry Soda Lake. By turning up the sod a small quantity of fresh water was found, though highly alkaline. Whipple wrote, "For an emigrant

Cinder cone and corral in the Mojave National Preserve   PHOTO: Wynne Benti

road, it is probably the best route yet discovered across this western desert."

After another twelve miles in the morning, they reached the Mojave River, "'a beautiful stream of fresh water, ten to twenty feet wide and a foot deep." They followed the intermittent stream to the foot of Sierra San Bernardino, then on into the Los Angeles basin.

Whipple wrote very favorably of the "Mohave Valley" and its fine potential for farming, saying "The Mormons made a great mistake in not occupying the valley of the Colorado."

After the Indians attacked a caravan on the banks of the Colorado, Secretary Jeff Davis ordered scouting of a road, west from Fort Defiance, by Lieutenant Beale of the Camel Corps. Fort Mohave was established in 1859, and then a string of camps followed along the Old Government Road. An adobe fort was built at Las Vegas, while a base camp, Camp Cady, was built near Daggett. Major Carlton built a fort in the Piute Mountains, which he named Fort Beale.

To provide for escort riders, posts were established at Soda Springs, Marl Springs, Rock Spring and Pah-Ute Creek. In 1868, the better Bradshaw Road was broken from San Gorgonio to La Paz on the Colorado River. Peace had been established with the Native Americans, and in 1871 the deserted buildings of the posts were sold and the last soldiers—caretakers—departed.

After the 1849 discovery of gold in California, mining expanded into the desert regions. But the first mines in the Mojave preceeded not only the '49ers but even the Mohaves, possibly by the ancestors of the Aztecs on their way to Mexico. Pits of turquoise mines, with ancient tools, have been found near Turquoise Mountain (Toltec Mine) and Ivanpah. Local Paiutes have no recollection of early mining on their lands.

The two best known areas are the Randsburg-Red Mountain complex and that surrounding Calico, now a county park.

In the Eastern Mojave area, what is now Mojave National Preserve, locations were first made in the New York and Providence Mountains in 1863, followed by the Rock Spring and Clark mining districts. The Bonanza King near Providence was discovered in the 1880s, and produced some $60,000,000 in silver. This kind of money paid for new railroads.

The "boom years" of mining in northeastern San Bernardino County were 1900-1919 when copper, lead and zinc was discovered in addition to gold and silver. After World War I, mines faltered and the miners fell on hard times. The War Act of WW II shut down almost all the rest. The Vulcan Mine, near Foshay Pass continued to produce iron ore. Non-metallics, clay, talc, and cinders as well as the "rare earths," used in electronic development, continue to be active.

Following page: Mojave National Preserve   PHOTO: Wynne Benti

A word about safety

Without the proper equipment and preparation, traveling in the desert can be a dangerous activity, so it is reasonable to assume that certain risks and hazards are associated with traveling and hiking in the remote desert regions of California and Nevada. Some of these hazards include, but are not limited to: vehicle brekdown, adverse weather conditions, unpredictable flash floods, stream crossings, sand drifts, loose rock and rockfall, rugged terrain, contact with native wildlife, hypothermia, heat stroke and heat exhaustion, hyponatremia and dehydration. Carry plenty of water. Let someone know your travel plans, where you are going, and when you plan to return. Make sure your vehicle is in good running condition, with at least one good spare, and a basic tool kit. Stay on established roads! Do not cut new tracks! The author and publisher of this guide make no representations as to the safety of any driving or hiking route described in this book. Always check ahead for pertinent information, as conditions are constantly changing. There is no substitute for knowledge of safety procedures and a little common sense.

A word about archaeological sites and artifacts

Archaeological sites and artifacts are protected by the Antiquities Act of 1906 and the Archaeological Resources Protection Act of 1979. All historic and prehistoric sites on federal lands are protected and defacement, removal, excavation or destruction of such antiquities is prohibited by law.

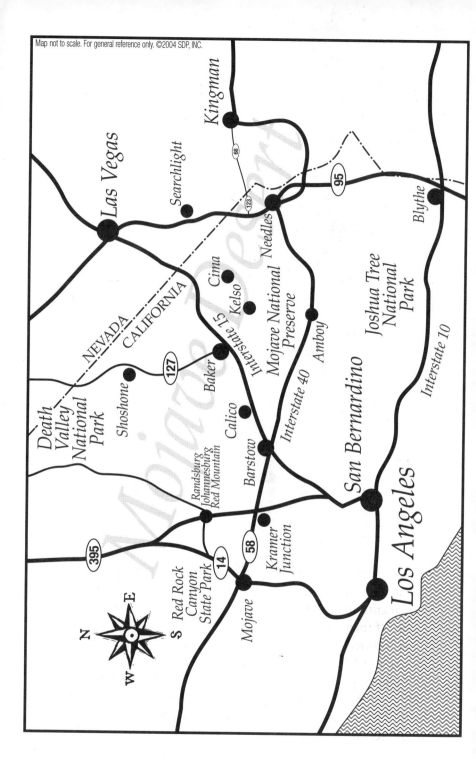

RANDSBURG
JOHANNESBURG
RED MOUNTAIN & ATOLIA

Red Mountain and Atolia   PHOTO: Wynne Benti

The old mines and workings of Red Mountain along Highway 395 are quiet now, part of the Mojave Desert's colorful past. The settlement's main street faces Red Mountain, hence the town's name. If there could be such a thing, it is also a roaring ghost town, infused with the lore of its distant sisters, Goldfield, Calico and Rhyolite. Broken-down shacks, rusted headworks and a few rugged residents are all that's left of this old town. Up until the 1950s like many rural California towns, Red Mountain had a brothel. Buses with the football players from rural high school teams stopped for pop and snacks at a store along Red

The Glamis/Rand Mining Corporation ziggurat   PHOTO: Wynne Benti

Mountain's highway frontage. The ladies at the brothel loved to wander over and tease the young men, only to be run off by the bus driver and chaperones.

Directly behind the town lies Kelly Silver mine. To the south is Atolia, where great quantities of tungsten and molybdenum were mined. In Johannesburg to the north and Randsburg to the west, are numerous gold and silver mines, and beyond these, lies Mojave's golden ore beds.

The Red Mountain mines that sat idle for years began operating around the clock in the 1940s to supply the increased demands of the War Department for tungsten, molybdenum and potash. Water in those busy times sometimes sold for as much as one cent per gallon, but a good dinner from soup to apple pie was only fifty cents. The 1940 mining camp population was comparable to the wild 1920s, when the rich vein that led to the town's founding was discovered.

The camps of Johannesburg (locally called "Joburg") and Randsburg were similar settlements, but possessed more water,

Randsburg's Main Street   PHOTO: Wynne Benti

railroad spurs and wider streets. The principal mine in old Randsburg was the Yellow Aster, extracting millions of dollars worth of gold. Her glory hole was 1,200 feet deep, with walls of granite and schist. Today, Glamis Gold/Rand Mining Corporation operates the mine, the giant ziggurat towering over the town.

In the Stringer Mining District to the south of Red Mountain were ten or more mines with small-veined, but rich ore. Atolia, along with an abundance of molybdenum, was also one of the largest producers of scheelite, an ore in the tungsten family. At the "Spud Patch" loose ore found in potato-shaped chunks was dug up and mined by hand. Later, power shovels removed the tungsten-bearing soil and exposed veins of valuable ore in the bedrock.

Red Rock Canyon State Park is a short distance southwest of these mining camps on Highway 14. A symphony of eroded red and white volcanic rock, fantastic forms have been carved by the wind, rain and seismic upheaval. From dawn to dusk it is an ever-changing picture of shimmering shadows.

Red Rock Canyon   PHOTO: Wynne Benti

Literally hundreds of dirt trails lead to forgotten mines, desolate canyons and remarkable landscapes. An exploration of these old mining camps with the added bonus of the scenic splendor of Red Rock Canyon make for a rewarding desert trails excursion.

Directions: Take CA-14 for 19.6 miles north of the town of Mojave, past Jawbone Canyon. Turn right on the paved Red Rock-Randsburg Road for 21 miles to Randsburg. Turn right for one mile to Johannesburg, or left for 3 miles to Red Mountain, both on US-395. Atolia is three miles south of Red Mountain on 395.

From Las Vegas take I-15 to Barstow. Exit west on CA-58 for 35.7 miles to Kramer Junction. Turn right on 395 and drive 26 miles to Atolia, followed by Red Mountain, Johannesburg and Randsburg.

Directions to Red Rock Canyon State Park: From the town of Mojave, Red Rock Canyon State Park is approximately 25 miles north on CA-14, or about 5 miles north of the Red Rock-Randsburg Road junction with CA-14. There is an excellent visitor center with museum, campground and miles and miles of trails. Many dirt roads lead to old mines and springs and will provide years of exploration. [4WD]

Maps: AAA Kern County, DeLorme's Southern California Atlas & Gazetteer

C A L I C O
BLACK MOUNTAINS WILDERNESS & RAINBOW BASIN
—‡—

In the late 1880s, most of California's mining camps were difficult to access, but not Calico. With the discovery of silver in 1881, settlers build the railroad station at Daggett, just eight miles away and accessible via a relatively negotiable road. By the standards of the rough-and-tumble boom towns of the Wild West, Calico was never a particularly rough camp. Of the 2000 miners and their families who lived here, only one citizen was lost to gunplay in the town's first year. Over 60 million dollars of silver was produced in Calico.

The town was quite picturesque in comparison to other camps of the 1880s; even its newspaper had a quaint, homey name: The Calico Print. But it was also incredibly hot during the summer. To escape the triple-digit summer heat, folks lived inside old mine tunnels.

The Calico Hills are covered with extensive workings. The Silver King Mine in Odessa Canyon produced ten million dollars in silver alone. Other high-grade mines included the Bismark, Garfield, Red Jacket, Run Over and Waterloo. A small railroad took the ore to Daggett for processing. At one time Calico boasted three mills with a total of 105 stamps.

After the high-grade silver slacked out and the price of precious ore dropped, Calico was for the most part deserted, and for many years remained just another Western ghost town, visited by the occasional Sunday desert explorer from Southern California and Nevada. Then in 1951, Walter Knott of Knott's Berry Farm fame, acquired the town from the Zenda Mining

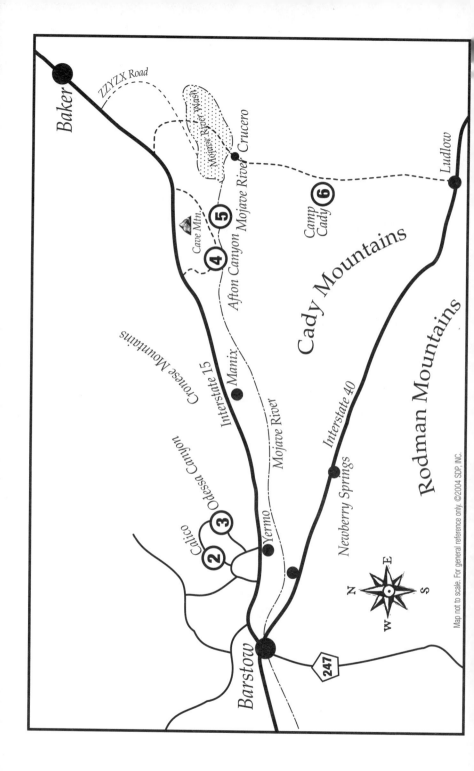

Map not to scale. For general reference only. ©2004 SDP, INC.

Calico Main Street PHOTO: Leslie Payne

Company and began to restore Calico to its original frontier splendor, hoping to establish a desert tourist attraction. Losing interest, Knott donated Calico to the County of San Bernardino in 1965, to serve as a county park.

Wall Street Canyon, just above Calico, is lovely. The rock colors offer a profusion of pastel hues to delight the eye, and there exist enough remaining mine tailings in the area to provide hours of interest to mineral enthusiasts. Near Calico, just north of Barstow, lies a large fossil bed (a federally protected site) and outcropping of petroglyphs.

Leading anthropologists have conducted extensive work at Rainbow Basin National Natural Landmark over the years. The scientific digs yielded camel bones dating back eleven millions years. These chalky, multi-colored bluffs were home to many other ancient discoveries. West and south of Rainbow Basin are Black and Inscription Canyons in the Black Mountains Wilderness area with some of the most beautiful and peaceful desert scenery in Southern California.

Directions to Calico: Take I-15 east from Barstow, to the Calico Road exit and follow the signs north to Calico Ghost Town Regional Park. There is a fee to enter the park (as of press time adults $6; kids 6-15, $5; children under five are free). Many events all year including a weekend eve ghost walk. [2WD]

To Rainbow Basin National Natural Landmark: From the intersection of old State Route 58 and Irwin Road in Barstow head north a few miles on Irwin Road to the signed Fossil Bed Road and turn west, left. Drive about three miles to Rainbow Basin National Natural Landmark (signed) and turn right. Just up ahead, the road forks: left goes to the one-way loop through Rainbow Basin; right goes to Owl Campground. The roads are graded dirt and accessible with careful driving in a passenger vehicle. Be warned: Fort Irwin is next door and the concussion from pretty big explosives can be felt at both places. [2WD]

To Black Mountains Wilderness Area Loop: Bring your DeLorme Gazetteer for this beautiful drive through spectacular desert country, a 53 mile loop from the intersection of the Copper City and Irwin Roads back to Rainbow Basin. Follow the directions above to Fossil Bed Road and continue an additional mile past Fossil Bed Road to Copper City Road and turn left, northwest. Drive about 16.4 miles to the junction of Copper City and Indian Springs Road (straight ahead). Jog hard left on Copper City and stay left at forks, the idea being to get to the base of the mesa and hug it until you reach Black Canyon about 28.4 miles (at 24.7 miles you'll see the BLM Black Mountains Wilderness sign). At 36.4 miles (well out of the canyon) pass another BLM Black Mountain Wilderness sign and turn on the road to your left, which passes by a ranch. Follow this road (EF401) back to Rainbow Basin at approximately 52.2 miles. Do not drive these roads after a rain—wait a few days as the roads are slick, flooded and impassable! [4WD required!]

Maps: AAA San Bernardino County, DeLorme's Southern California Atlas & Gazetteer

Opposite: Inside Rainbow Basin National Natural Landmark loop. PHOTO: Wynne Benti

ODESSA AND MULE CANYONS
OLD MOHAVIA AND A HIKE UP CALICO PEAK
— ❋ —

Most Westerners have at least heard of Calico, the restored ghost town lying ten miles northeast of Barstow. For years the sun burnt shacks of the old mining camp have sagged amidst barren hills and dry, brittle ground whose vivid hues are a result of the mineral pigmentation of the soil itself. But in prehistoric times, Calico was practically a seaside resort on the western edge of a land mass geologists have named Mohavia, as many of the typical aspects of the formation are found near the central portion of the Mojave Desert.

For ages all was serene in the wooded hills and plains of old Mohavia, herds of three-toed horses and early American camels roamed. Forces deep within the earth's crust began to stir. Massive faults formed and the land broke into huge blocks and ridges that rose and buckled and eventually sunk.

Rivers that once freely drained the uplands for millions of years, were now stopped by the rising mountain ranges and enormous gravel beds formed the basins made by the settling fault blocks. These basins were something like the dry lakes of today. Rain washes and landslides contributed debris from the mountainsides to the growing beds of sediment, resulting in a formation thousands of feet thick. These strata contained rock fragments of all sizes, from massive boulders to fine silt.

Near Calico, weather has carved the strata into a complex assortment of hills and gullies that make up Odessa Canyon.

Opposite: Scouting the crux maneuver at the Odessa Narrows   PHOTO: Wynne Benti

The ground comes in a variety of colors, ranging from yellow, brown, green, orange, red and even blue and lavender. Curiously-pigmented rocks are to be found by the thousands as loose pebbles, cobbles and boulders on the alluvial fans sloping away toward Calico Dry Lake. It is as if these stones await discovery by rock hounds.

Some of the rocks and pebbles clearly have been carried from distant sources. There are such specimens as green epidote and rounded hunks of brown and red quartzite, which are probably cobbles from some distant beach. Many have been so pulverized, re-pulverized and again cemented that the best identification is to call them sandstones, arkoses, hardened mud, climes and claystone. They include shades of bright green, bluish-green, blue the exact color of faded denim, as well as warm shades of yellows and red.

The red pigment in a typical sample of Calico jasper consists of ferric oxide in the form of powdery hematite or red ocher. This is the source of all the red shades from pink to reddish-purple, but ferric oxide in other combinations also make another set of warm colors—yellows, oranges and browns.

There is another series of iron oxides, the ferrous oxides, which generally produce some shade of green or greenish-black and some combinations forming blue compounds. The blue mudstone mentioned earlier looks as if it might contain copper, but tests have shown the only pigment to be iron. Combinations of the two types of iron oxide in the same rock produce unusual shades such as bronze, yellowish-green and olive. There are also numerous deposits of yellow jasper in Odessa Canyon.

So when you admire the fantastically bent and colored strata and the vivid rocks of Odessa Canyon in the hills north of Barstow, you'll be looking upon the evidence of the violent chemistry and geologic upheavals. These events produced jasper and multitudes of other rocks along the alluvial fans near Calico Mountain and Odessa Canyon.

Directions: From Barstow take I-15 east from Barstow towards Las Vegas about 11 miles to the Yermo/Ghost Town Road exit. At the end of the exit turn north and drive approximately 2.2 miles to signed Doran Scenic Drive and turn right. This area has been taken over by OHVers so the once beautiful canyon, which still has its color, has been eroded into worn-down nubs. The canyon drive is short, ending on the other side of a narrow passage that is well worth the trip. After that, only the brave dare climb the rocky crux manuever into the main canyon. The publisher of this book has seen the damage done to 4WD vehicles attempting to climb this rocky route. They do it, but we do not recommend it! Mule Canyon is a much nicer alternate route through terrain similar to that found in Odessa Canyon.

Alternate scenic drive up Mule Canyon and hike up Calico Peak: From I-15, take the Yermo/Ghost Town Road and drive north 0.8 miles on Ghost Town Road to Mule Canyon Road. Turn right and drive up Mule Canyon through colorful hills 1.5 miles to a fork. Stay right and continue two miles through badland hills, crossing a divide and dropping to another junction. Turn left, and continue 3.6 miles west, climbing a rough, loose grade where four-wheel drive is recommended, to another junction. Turn north (right) and continue 0.4 miles to the locked gate at 3,200 feet. Most of the route is driveable to all vehicles. However, the steep hill will stop many two-wheel drive vehicles. One could easily walk the extra couple of miles to the locked gate from here though.

Route: Walk past the locked gate, and follow the steep road to the microwave station on the summit. Anticipate six miles round-trip with 1,400 feet of elevation gain from the locked gate. Hiking from the steep grade will add some significant mileage and elevation gain, but will still make for a fine, winter dayhike.

Maps: AAA San Bernardino County, DeLorme's Southern California Atlas & Gazetteer

The Mojave Road to Afton Canyon two days after a winter rain. PHOTO: Wynne Benti

AFTON CANYON
LISTEN TO THE LONESOME TRAINS WHISTLE
— ✳ —

Twenty miles northeast of Yermo, the rolling desert gives way to a terrain of extremely rugged character, lying between Cave Mountain on the north and Cady Mountains to the south. The high ground extending between the two ranges formed a barrier which undoubtedly damned the water of the Mojave River in bygone ages, but a weak section finally yielded to the erosive forces of pent-up waters and a gorge eventually formed. Today there are few places in the Mojave Desert that so graphically illustrate the results of erosion as Afton Canyon.

Near the entrance to this chasm the Mojave River rises to the surface and winds through a meadow dotted with course grass and verdant shrubbery. This expanse is covered with a white deposit, indicating the alkaline nature of the water, acquired by the leaching of desert soils through which it flows. One mile below the Afton railroad siding of the Union Pacific railway, a spur of the mountain has forced the river to form a great "U", which railroad engineers, loathing to deviate from straight lines, pierced with a tunnel. Debouching to the right before crossing the bridge, one may follow the course of the river and view the amazing rock formations lining the canyon walls.

A short distance below the bridge, a yawning cave, which gave the mountain its name, appears at the base of a towering mass of igneous rock. Fragments of bedding, cooking utensils and crockery suggest that perhaps some prospector camped here long ago. Beyond the cave –are great walls of sandstone, a material that readily lends itself to the vagaries of erosion.

Tributary canyons piercing the hills to the south show some marvelous examples of erosion, time's most elemental sculpture.

The lower portions of Afton Canyon are characterized by infinite varieties of rock masses. Light sandstone ends abruptly at a great igneous uplift, almost black in color, which is streaked with brown, blue, pink and white. Harder than sandstone, it is much more resistant to erosion, but lacks the ornate detail seen in the softer rock. With its bizarre colors, however, this fire-born rock seems even stranger. The barren country of this region has changed little across the ages. But through the vast silence of a desert night, faint whispers seem discernable; perhaps the crackle of an Indian campfire, the musical lilt of Castilian voices, or the rattle and creak of ox-drawn wagons. The spell remains until a new sound steals through—the drone of an airplane winging its way under the stars or the Union Pacific engines pulling their heavy loads across the desert grades.

Directions: Take I-15 35.6 miles past Barstow to the Afton Canyon exit and head south on graded dirt. At 2.9 miles there is a fork. To the right, on the other side of the train bridge is the continuation of the westbound Mojave Road and the Mojave River riparian habitat currently in the process of restoration—excellent bird watching opportunities here. The left fork goes to the campground and to Afton Canyon, approximately 5.3 miles from I-15 to the entrance to the canyon. The Union Pacific tracks are active all night long so don't expect a quiet night's sleep!

Afton Canyon to Basin Road Scenic Loop: Continue east through the canyon along the Old Mojave Road that parallels the tracks (in and out of the wash) to the railroad siding of Basin. The road turns north away from the tracks and is followed around Cave Mountain about ten miles to I-15. Return to Afton Canyon by southbound I-15. Don't travel these roads right after rains—they *will* be impassable. [4WD]

Maps: AAA San Bernardino County, DeLorme's Southern California Atlas & Gazetteer

MOJAVE RIVER
WATER EVERYWHERE AND NOWHERE

Within the far-reaching borders of the Great American Desert, there is no natural feature so abounding in contradictions as the Mojave River. In most respects it differs from other waterways on this continent, behaving in a manner quite contradictory to normal steam phenomena.

The waters have their origin in the San Bernardino Mountains where melting snow, rains and crystal springs find their way into pine-clad valleys and rocky chasms that bound its tributary forks. With a length of but 90 miles, rising and dying totally within the San Bernardino Country, the Mojave River transverses an extraordinary route and, unlike practically all of its brethren, empties into a broad playa where evaporation is so rapid that water seldom accumulates enough to form a lake.

The manner in which its waters survive the onslaught of the desert sun is no doubt the most remarkable of the river's idiosyncrasies. An apt comparison might be that of a small army marching through hostile territory where well-organized snipers take heavy toll of its numbers, as the rate of evaporation in the California desert is approximately seven feet per year. The only defense, then, is concealment beneath sands and gravel covering the bed of the channel. Along a major portion of the length of this remarkable river its waters take refuge under the coarse alluvium, emerging only in a few places where dikes or rock force them to the surface. Here is a peculiar case in which the bottom of a stream is on top—literally a river turned upside-down!

The Mojave River PHOTO: LESLIE PAYNE

Rarely do floods of sufficient volume flow down the channel to inundate the bed of the Mojave for its entire length. Ordinarily spring freshets are swallowed up by the sands before they reach Yermo or Daggett.

The upper reaches of the Mojave, starting at the base of the San Bernardino Mountains, have steep gradients, and here the stream bed is covered with eroded cobblestones. Where foothills merge into desert, the slope of the channel flattens out and stones and pebbles give way to sand. Out on the wide expanse of the desert itself, where the slope is still flatter, flood waters are so diminished in velocity that their burden of sand does not escape the bed of the river, which is therefore gradually building up to higher levels. In this respect it differs from most rivers, whose currents constantly scour deeper.

The course of the Mojave River remains as remote as in ages past. Deep sand washes, muddy expanses, secret oases of greenery and the remains of mines and settlements long deserted, make the flow of the Mojave interesting to follow.

Soda Lake is the final stage of the Mojave River. Desert nomenclature is misleading, with most of its lakes lacking the one element to make the terminology correct—water! Soda Lake differs little from others of its kind dotting the desert. It is a great playa, fifteen miles long and seven miles wide, level as a floor and covered with a white deposit, rich with the chemical contents of the water draining into the Mojave River basin for ages. As the lake's name indicates, the composition of this deposit is largely sodium carbonate with a variety of other alkalis present, as well.

Thus ends the tale of the Mojave, strangest of rivers. Rising and sinking, only 90 miles long, yet possessing a relatively large annual flow, the river remains one of the desert's many enigmas.

Directions: Take I-15 past Barstow for 35.8 miles to the Afton Canyon exit and turn south to the campground. Just before the train bridge, take the left fork to the campground, the eastbound Mojave Road. The right fork is the westbound Mojave Road and continues under the train bridge. Pass the campground on your left (a second train bridge on your right) and follow the the Mojave Road through Afton Canyon, the Mojave River wash. Drive to the Basin railroad stop, then cross the Mojave River Sink (often flooded in winter and impassable), to Crucero, where the road turns north. Follow the road to the edge of Soda Dry Lake. It is not possible to make the short loop through ZZYZX back to I-15 as it has been closed for research. [4WD]

Map: AAA San Bernardino County, DeLorme's Southern California Atlas & Gazetteer

Camp Cady today   PHOTO: WYNNE BENTI

CAMP CADY
BATTLE-BORN OF THE MOJAVE

The placement of Camp Cady was highly strategic, at the junction of the two major routes to Southern California. The first, and by the far the oldest route, was charted by Father Francisco Garces in 1775 and later became the high road between Santa Fe and the Pacific and the only mail route between California and the Arizona territory.

The second road, known as the Mormon Trail, was explored by adherent of Joseph Smith and used by them as a way between their metropolis of Salt Lake City and their distant colony at San Bernardino.

Camp Cady was battle-born and the focal point of many campaigns, long and arduous patrols, attacks and counter-attacks during its brief career. These skirmishes were relatively minor in the greater context of the efforts by Anglo settlers to settle the West; but for the citizens of Los Angeles, beleaguered by Indian attacks on trade caravans, these fights took on the significance of more legendary battles, such as the infamous Battle of Bull Run.

In May, 1860 the United States Army dispatched to the Mojave Sector, Major James H. Carleton and a detachment of First Dragoons from Fort Tejon, to establish a permanent garrison and visit retribution on Paiute Indians who did not comply with the Anglo settlers' rule of law.

Near Soda Lake, the sink of the Mojave River, several bands of Native Americans made their temporary homes. The spot was particularly suited to ambush—a wide, flat area where large mesquite trees grew in profusion and offered cover from which wagon trains and scouting parties could be observed. The military confronted the indigenous population and several battles ensued. Major Carleton and his troops, with their superior firepower, delivered a powerful demonstration of military strength. Paiute leaders were deeply impressed and agreed to peace without delay.

With the brokering of peace, travel became safer and Carleton's soldiers returned to Fort Tejon. During this time a small defense fort, was constructed at Camp Cady, another at Bitter Spring on the Salt Lake Road, and a third at Soda Lake. In addition a number of springs were opened and reservoirs built to hold large supplies of water.

The Mojave Desert, by its very nature, continued to be a dangerous region. Hostilities between the new settlers and Native Americans ranged far and wide. The need for a garrison remained and Camp Cady was permanently occupied until 1871, when peace was finally established. The last soldier stationed at the camp, Lieutenant James Halloran of the Twelfth Infantry, superintended the sale of government equipment and property and the installation of Cantwell and Winters, stockmen, as new owners.

Camp Cady was reduced by the elements to a picturesque ruin. In 1989, when this book was first written, remnants of the old barracks stood silent, their walls deteriorating a little more with each passing rain. Beneath a giant, gnarled cottonwood were the walls of an old guardhouse. Other structures had long vanished with the old parade ground becoming the pasture for livestock, successors to the cavalry steeds of yesteryear. Today, a historic sign marks the spot.

Directions: Take I-15 north from Barstow 24 miles to Harvard Road and exit, heading south. At 0.8 miles turn left (east) on Cherokee Road. Drive approximately 2.6 miles, eventually along a fence, to its end, then turn right (south) 0.75 mile to north bank of the Mojave River. The Camp Cady Ranch is owned by the California State Department of Fish and Game and butts up against other private property. The California State historic marker is accessible and marks the approximate site location.

Map: AAA San Bernardino County, DeLorme's Southern California Atlas & Gazetteer

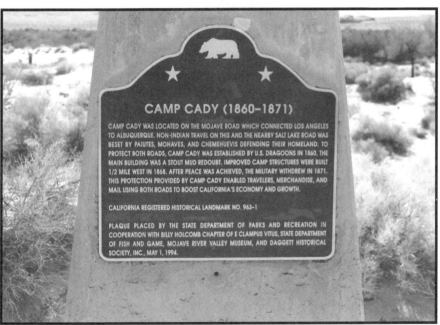

PHOTO: WYNNE BENTI

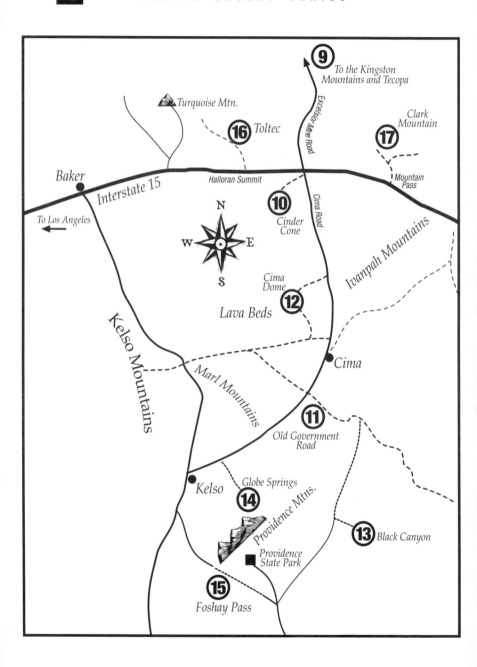

9 To the Kingston
Mountains and Tecopa

Turquoise Mtn.

16 Toltec

Excelsior Mine Road

Clark
Mountain

17

Baker

Interstate 15

Halloran Summit

Mountain
Pass

To Los Angeles

10
Cinder
Cone

Cima Road

Ivanpah Mountains

N

W   E

S

Cima
Dome

12

Lava Beds

Kelso Mountains

Marl Mountains

Cima

11
Old Government
Road

Kelso

Globe Springs

14

Providence Mtns.

13 Black Canyon

Providence
State Park

15

Foshay Pass

ANCIENT OCEANS
OF THE MOJAVE
WARM INLAND SEAS

Now regarded as desolate, an area twelve miles from Baker contains the evidence of ancient seas that once covered the Mojave Desert millions of years ago, proof this region once teemed with life. The road there presents no great difficulties. North from I-15 at Baker, CA 127 crosses the Mojave Wash. Skirting a small range of mountains, it swings northwesterly toward Death Valley. Approximately ten miles past the site of Silver Lake, a little-used road branches to the right towards the ruins of Riggs and the Silurian Hills, across a broad alluvial slope that extends from the mountain to the south. Occasional cross-washes make speed impossible, and one dry watercourse of large proportions lies across the road, but the sand is not sufficiently deep to halt the process of four-wheel drive vehicles.

The surrounding country is characterized by soft contours and sweeping lines that indicate a rather slow but uniform action by elemental forces, constantly at work leveling valleys and covering hills. As the trail bears to the right and descends to the floor of a broad wash, one becomes aware of a change. Here is an extensive tableland, ending abruptly on the south in an imposing array of cliffs, pinnacles, shoulders and escarpments, pierced at intervals by deep recesses.

Following a serpentine course between the low hills, the wash branches out into several smaller channels which then become lost in rockbound canyons. Here and there a yucca rears its thorny branches above the stunted greasewood.

Vegetation is scarce, as the shallow soil overlying the strata of stone holds little moisture and offers scant covering for roots. The charm of this corner of the Mojave Desert is indeed in its geology, rather than its vegetation.

Incredible as it seems, after the oceans evaporated, this region was clothed in plant life and abounded with fauna. Paleontologists have recovered numerous fossils laid bare by erosion: a camel closely related to the South American llama, two species of the three-toed horse, the giraffe camel and a small antelope. They also found fossil records of a large creature that is a connecting link between the dog and bear families. Another of these "dogs", far larger than any domestic variety, had a skull over a foot in length. The formation in which these fossils were found is the Upper Miocene era, which geologists estimate was laid down some 25 million years ago.

Beyond a high, rocky ridge forming the eastern boundary of the sculptured cliffs, is a separate valley distinctive in appearance. In the absence of the massive sandstone, thousands of trickling streams from infrequent rains have cut wrinkles in the hillside. Where the streams combined in large volume, the rifts deepened and widened into tiny canyons—a miniature stretch of badlands—a desolate scene, of mystery and grandeur.

Directions: Take I-15 north to Baker, then turn left on the Death Valley Highway, CA-127. Pass the site of Silver Lake at about 10.9 miles. Continue another 10 miles and turn right on a poor dirt road that heads east into the Silurian Hills. Go 7.9 miles to the fossils beds of the ancient seas. From Las Vegas, drive south on I-15 to Baker, then turn right on the Death Valley Highway. [4WD]

Maps: AAA San Bernardino County, DeLorme's Southern California Atlas & Gazetteer

Ship of the Desert
GHOSTLY FORMS HAUNT THE SANDY SEAS

Truth, they say, is stranger than fiction, and what could be stranger than a sailing ship riding arid waves of sand? Such a legend has persisted for more than a hundred years. Here are four separate stories that have stood the test of time:

The year was 1867. Prospectors Dusty Miller and Duke Chellow hesitated at the mouth of a narrow valley. Was the tall masted apparition at which they gazed only a mirage? It did not waver, however, but stood solid against the stark background. Can you imagine what went on in the minds of those awe-stricken prospectors as they came into full view of the half-buried prow? A ship of the desert? Where, when and how did this ghostly ship sail on a sea of sand?

One explanation is as follows: In the spring of 1861 William H. Perry of Los Angeles was commissioned to build a six-foot scow capable of navigating the treacherous Colorado River. The completed scow was roped securely on a large ox-drawn wagon. It crossed the San Gorgonio Pass without incident and headed for the deep desert. Constantly plagued by lack of water and heavy sand, they bogged down for the final time. Already tilted from the uneven surface of the canyon, the trim scow slipped off the wagon to be abandoned and buried by decades of wind-blown sand. The extreme aridity of the desert preserved the wood and throughout the years, the wind that covered the ship also uncovered it, time and time again.

A ship of the desert? PHOTO: LESLIE PAYNE

Another tale about a desert ship originates in the 1870s, when an iron steamer, THE EXPLORER, was torn from its mooring on the Colorado River by an unusually fierce storm. This vessel, intended for exploration of the Colorado, had been assembled in Port Isabel in 1857. Lieutenant Joseph Ives assumed command of THE EXPLORER and steamed up the Colorado River from its mouth to Black Canyon, near the future site of Hoover Dam. Later the little steamer was also used for local traffic until its loss. Battered and broken, the ship seemed to have vanished into thin air. During ensuing years the lost ship became a legend encrusted with the lore of twice-told tales. In 1930 it was reported to have been seen on the Sonora side of the river. Later fragments were found in an overgrown thicket on the lower Colorado Delta.

In 1933 a ship was sighted half-buried in the Mojave Desert, this time by a pair of botanists examining the desert floor for certain specimens of cacti. As they entered a deep canyon, they were astounded to see the prow of an old ship jutting from a cliff. Weathered with age, it shone with a silvery glow. The climb to the top of the cliff would be almost perpendicular, requiring special equipment. They decided to return to town and seek help in scaling the cliff.

On the very day of their return, the tremendous Long Beach earthquake shook all of Southern California. The canyon containing the ship crumbled under the seismic jolt. The force of the first shock threw the couple to the ground. Regaining their feet, they looked up to see their fantastic discovery was now buried under tons of rock and gravel, where it still remains.

There are many other tales of ghostly ships haunting our deserts, and even records to support the most persistent stories. A cache of gold is what most adventurers seek, and who knows what treasures may lie in the hull of a long-lost vessel? But perhaps the discovery and photographic documentation of such a ship would have its own rewards for a desert adventurer.

Directions: Take I-15 to Baker, then turn north on CA-127 (towards Death Valley) for 20.2 miles. A dirt road leads west for 13.7 miles to the area where the ship was last sighted. Pack a nice lunch, water and enjoy the scenery (not to mention, good luck)!

From Las Vegas, take I-15 south to Arden-Blue Diamond turnoff (NV 180). After 38 miles take Tecopa cut-off (Old Spanish Trail) to Tecopa. Then, take the Baker Highway (CA-127) south for 22 miles to the above turnoff, and west 13.1 miles to the possible site.

Maps: AAA San Bernardino County, DeLorme's Southern California Atlas & Gazetteer

Ruins on the Excelsior Mine Road, heading north to the Kingston Mountains from I-15
PHOTO: WYNNE BENTI

KINGSTON MOUNTAINS
AN UNLIKELY OASIS

Grazing at Horse Thief Springs PHOTO: LESLIE PAYNE

The Kingston Mountains are known for their excellent hiking and amethyst crystals, but few desert wanderers are aware of sleepy Horse Thief Springs.

The Kingstons are sharply divided by a deep canyon separating the southern portion from the northern part. A fault, running east and west, serves as a channel to carry water from a series of springs. Westernmost is a spring located at the Smith Talc Mine. Next appears Crystal Springs at the Silver Rule Mine, then Beck Springs at the Standard Slag Iron Mine. The eastern-

Bishop artist, Richard Coons, explores Horse Thief Springs PHOTO: WYNNE BENTI

most spring is called Horse Thief, which serves as headquarters for a cattle ranch.

Lying just inside the California border in the extreme northeast corner of San Bernardino County, Horse Thief Springs provided rest and grazing for stolen animals being hastily driven over the Mojave Desert. Irate Mexicans pursued the thieves to the Kingston Mountains, but never dared to enter this isolated mountain range.

In 1829, Antonio Armijo, a trader from Santa Fe, set out on a trading expedition to San Gabriel and blazed a route henceforth known as the "Spanish Trail." Returning to Santa Fe with a large herd of horses, which he had received in exchange for his merchandise, he set the stage for this to become an annual occasion. Horses multiplied on California grasslands to such an extent that they threatened the range. It became necessary to hold roundups. Thus Armijo's route was soon well-worn by vaqueros.

Others followed Armijo's trail. Large caravans of merchandise went west over this route to California and in the spring when the land was green with tender grasses and shrubs, large herds of horses were driven back over it. In 1842 one band on record consisted of over 4,000 head, moving eastbound from southern California. In between legal drives, thieves made regular stops at the spring and master thief, Pegleg Smith, was a frequent visitor. One of the last hauls was made in 1845, when 1800 head were watered here.

When horse thieves ceased to use the springs, only an occasional prospector or Indian traveler visited the little oasis until the arrival of the Lee brothers in the mid-1870s. The Lees were cattlemen and followed the mining strikes, supplying fresh beef for workers. One of the brothers, Cub Lee, ranged cattle all over the desert and mountains, even into Death Valley. At Horse Thief Springs he built a cabin and planted cottonwood trees that still tower over the springs and cover the acre of level ground secluded in a deep ravine.

Today there is an air of respectability over the Kingston Mountains. The tedious business of mining talc, iron and other minerals is carried on in an orderly manner. Huge trucks snake their way to the mines to haul away dazzling white talc from beneath peaks inhabited by mountain sheep, who often stand for hours, seemingly puzzling over what is going on below. In spite of these activities, however, there are still hidden canyons, just as quiet and remote as when Pegleg Smith and his boys whooped into camp after a successful raid on Mexican rancheros.

Directions: Take I-15 for 27 miles north of Baker to the Cima Road exit. Turn north on Cima Road (which immediately becomes Excelsior Mine Road north of I-15) for 23 miles to the mine spur. Three miles ahead, the spring is just off the road to the left, a lush green spot that is on private property (respect the no trespassing signs). For an interesting trip, continue on the road ahead and follow it past the big mine, all the way to Tecopa (with its mineral baths) and CA-127 which can be followed back to I-15 or to Shoshone and Death Valley.

From Las Vegas, take I-15 south for 38 miles to Jean. Turn west on the Goodsprings Road for 7 miles to the village. Turn left for 12 miles to Sandy. At the Sandy Mill, go south for 1.4 miles, then west on a dirt road. It is 13.6 miles to Horse Thief Springs in the Kingston Range, just short of the summit.
Map: AAA San Bernardino County, DeLorme's Southern California Atlas & Gazetteer

A CINDER CONE VALLEY
VOLCANIC CONES OVER 7 MILLION YEARS OLD
—— ✳ ——

Millions of years ago, our southwestern land was in constant upheaval due to fires deep within the earth's core. Great streams of molten lava burst forth from the earth's crust, and as the surface cooled, the eruptions left in their wake hundreds of small volcanic craters called cinder cones. Around the base of each formed a river of black stones.

Cinder Cone National Natural Landmark, east of Kelbaker Road and west of Cima, has 32 prime examples of nature on a rampage. The first of these volcanoes began their activity 7.6 million years ago, stopping only 10,000 years ago, at the end of the last major ice age. Everywhere the ground is strewn with serrated fragments of lava. These cones are covered with coarse, pitted cinders several feet thick. Imagine millions of tons of ash and cinder deposits from a furnace and you may begin to visualize how this awesome valley is.

The slopes to the cones' rims are steep, and the loose covering makes climbing almost an impossibility. For every step a climber takes, his feet sink a good 12 to 14 inches into the granules, but using a zigzag course, it is possible to reach the summit. There is little variation in the size and shape of these cones. They are some 200 to 300 feet across and several hundred feet high. Standing along the rim, gazing down into the strange funnel-shaped abyss, it is easy to picture the cone as a bubbling cauldron of molten lava.

Early Spanish explorers called the valley Lumbra Cerro (Fire Hill), while Indians cut a wide swath around this ominous region. In later days, prospectors had no fear of the valley. They scoured every inch of the territory searching for riches, but gold and silver are not found in the region. Surprisingly enough, there are a lot of mines throughout the lava beds with such unusual names as Paymaster, Oro Fino, Rainy Day and many others.

The valley remained untouched until modern man moved in his machines and began gouging deep holes into the flanks of these symmetrical cones. The cinders are used for road surfacing and have proven to be as valuable to their finders as the precious minerals would have been to the old prospectors. For the most part, however, Cinder Cone Valley remains the same—a primeval site hidden on the edges of a racing modern civilization.

It is a most unusual and rewarding spot. Winter months are a sheer delight. The sunshine glances off the ebony cones and generates warmth well into the afternoon. Try a picnic lunch, a leisurely stroll, an exerting climb to the lip of the cone or a walk to a prime example of a lava tube:

Directions: From Barstow, take I-15 north to Kelbaker Road. Exit and go south on Kelbaker about 20 miles. The cinder cones can be seen for miles.

Map: AAA San Bernardino County, DeLorme's Southern California Atlas & Gazetteer

CIMA DOME
DESERT VOLCANO

The Mojave Desert has always fascinated me. It is a land of anomalies, with each mile revealing a bit of history, Indian lore and strange and wonderful sights. One area that particularly appeals to my sense of exploration is Cima Dome.

The Dome is a geologic phenomenon, shaped like a huge inverted bowl. Its mineral composition consists principally of porphytic quartz monzonite, which disintegrates at a rapid pace, leaving projecting knobs, hillocks and ridges on the flanks of the dome that are composed of other intrusive rocks. These outcroppings are all the more resistant to weathering and erosion.

It was during a period of erosion, perhaps in late Pleistocene Era, that produced a huge surface of low relief on the granite rock of the Mojave Desert. At this time Cima Dome appeared as having exceptional smoothness, like a bubble covered with weathered granitic debris.

Seven miles southwest of the apex of Cima Dome lies another granite dome called Cimacito (Little Cima), a smaller version of the Cima Dome. The remains of several enozoic volcanoes perched on low hills dominate the southwestern and northwestern flanks of this smaller dome. These volcanic remnants suggest that Cimacito as well as Cima Dome were once partly covered by volcanoes. Prehistoric people living near Cima Dome used the basalt from these volcanic eruptions as grinding stones.

There are many four-wheel-drive roads that follow the flanks around the domes to the extensive volcanic fields nearby. On one

Cima PHOTO: WYNNE BENTI

of these roads leading toward Marl Spring is an outcropping of lovely crystalline rhyolite. There are several most interesting sites only a few miles from Cima Dome, one being Teutonia Peak and the Teutonia Silver Mine, just north of the peak.

The whole region is criss-crossed with old trails and roads used, no doubt, when power lines were put in from Hoover Dam to Los Angeles in the late 1930s and early 1940s. The entire country around Cima Dome is virtually an oasis in the booming San Bernardino County, a wonderful place to explore the interesting geologic formations.

Directions: Take I-15 for 40 miles north of Baker to the Cima Road exit. Turn right and drive approximately 18 miles to the townsite of Cima. Continue on for 4.4 miles to the Cedar Canyon Road then right to the dirt roads over and around the Dome. From Las Vegas, take I-15 south for 66 miles to the Cima off-ramp. There is a hiking trails off the road to Teutonia Peak with Cima as a side-trip.

Map: AAA San Bernardino County, DeLorme's Southern California Atlas & Gazetteer

The Old Government Road from Marl Springs PHOTO: LESLIE PAYNE

OLD GOVERNMENT ROAD
WAGONS HO!
—※—

Over 3,000 wagons a year, to be precise, came this way. The opening of the West beckoned hardy men and women from Oklahoma Territory across the mountains and deserts to California in 1854. They followed the route of Father Francisco Garces, who blazed a trail in 1775-76.

Several forts were erected along the way to offer some protection from hostile Paiute and Shoshone. Fort Mohave was one of the largest and the best equipped. The fort overlooked the Colorado River and its water and was a most welcome sight for parched humans and animals alike, after struggling over those long dry stretches.

From Fort Mohave they journeyed through Paiute Valley, replenishing water supplies at Sacramento Springs. The low Vontrigger Hills were crossed and travelers could again find water at Rock Springs in Round Valley. Cedar Canyon also offered cooling shade and water from several free-flowing springs. Camps around the springs were protected by small redoubts. Five of the dugouts and large foundations are still standing in Marl Springs and the water source that had been boxed in over a century ago, still trims with clear, cool water. Surprisingly, several early brass uniform buttons have been found in recent years on exploration trips to Marl Springs.

From Marl Springs the journey took travelers to Silver Lake and then to Soda Lake, both of which served as prehistoric encampments. In the Cronise Valley, the next stop along the route, many springs and campsites existed. All along the old road, survive wells and springs once used by those early travelers.

Father Garces returned east by a different route, going from Cedar Canyon to what is now Kelso, and over steep Foshay Pass, through Tennes Valley to Paiute Valley and finally to Fort Mohave. Most of the Old Government Road and the Father Garces Route are still visible.

The road twists and turns to avoid washes and gullies, but the rutted creases left by heavy wagons are easily followed in a four-wheel drive vehicle. The clearest part of the route is found on the Cima-Kelso Road, just 4.5 miles south of Cima. To the right, snakes a rutted trail through the low Marl Mountains. The arid floor of the desert grows verdant with vegetation around the clear, abundant Marl Springs water. Latter-day ranchers have erected several rude cattle holding pens, but for the most part, the road, campsites and springs remain as they were when pioneers and soldiers made that arduous trek over a century ago. [4WD]

Directions: From Barstow, take I-15 from 27 miles north of Baker to the Cima Road exit. Turn right, south, for 18 miles through the village of Cima and continue on towards Kelso for 4.4 miles. The Old Government Road turns right toward the Marl Mountains and left on the Cedar Canyon Road. From Las Vegas take I-15 south for 67 miles to the Cima Road exit.

Map: AAA San Bernardino County, DeLorme's Southern California Atlas & Gazetteer

BLACK CANYON
TEARS OF STONE
—❋—

The record of rocks is the very source book for geologists. It is an ancient volume, second only to the record book of the universe, and like all books of antiquity, it is fragmentary and difficult to decipher. When layers of sandstone, shale and limestone are deposited on top of one another, the lower is the oldest stratum. Rock that has been the longest exposed to the elements oftentimes develops a smooth, shiny, dark coating, called "patina" or "desert varnish." Entire mountains are often covered with these polished surfaces and they can also be found in small outcropping along canyon and basin floors.

In San Bernardino County, off Black Canyon Road, is an uneven, mountainous mass of hard, patina-covered rock. Many unusual cacti and desert succulents flourish here in the sandy loam. The dry stream bed glitters with small beads of black obsidian, commonly called "Apache Tears." Many legends have circulated about this name over the years. The following is just one of these tales:

The small frozen tear drops are the result of an Indian maiden's grief when her warrior lover climbed to the volcano's rim to chant an offering to the gods. She waited faithfully for his return and when the waiting days turned into years, she threw herself into the boiling cauldron, leaving only her tears, which turned to stone.

The canyon and stream terrace were favorite camping spots for many nomadic bands of Native Americans. Twenty years ago, slight blackened traces of their campfires were visible, with an abundance of chert chippings and flakes, a material used for making arrowheads. A prehistoric petroglyph depicting a pair of hands with outstretched fingers pointing downward has been interpreted as a danger or warning signal by today's rock art scholars.

On the highest ridge of the plateau, rises a magnificent view of Lanfair Valley, where winding trails look like yellow ribbons against a green carpet of vegetation. Wild burros, protected by state law, stare curiously at hikers and explorers, while a multitude of birds pepper the brilliant blue sky with pinpoints of color. A trip into Black Canyon is truly a rewarding experience.

The Black Canyon Road is good gravel. The trail is one mile past Hole-in-the-Wall Campground, then turn east. When passing through cattle gates, leave them as you find them. If you close a gate that a rancher has left open to allow stock to reach water, the stock will suffer. If a gate is closed, then you should of course close it as you pass through.

Directions: Take I-15 for 40 miles north of Baker to the Cima Road exit. Turn right for 18 miles to the village of Cima. Continue on for 4.4 miles to the Cedar Canyon Road. Turn left and continue 6.1 miles to Black Canyon. Head south for 9 miles to the petroglyph spur. The petroglyphs are approximately 7 miles to the east.

From Las Vegas drive south on I-15 for 66 miles to the Cima Road exit and follow instructions above.

Map: AAA San Bernardino County, DeLorme's Southern California Atlas & Gazetteer

At last
I shall give myself to the desert again,
that I, in its golden dust,
may be blown from a barren peak
broadcast over the sun-lands.

If you should desire some news of me,
go ask the little horned toad whose home is the dust,
or seek it among the fragrant sage,
or question the mountain juniper,
and, by their silence,
they will truly inform you.

Maynard Dixon's Epitaph, 1946

Old mine shaft near Globe Srpings   PHOTO: WYNNE BENTI

GLOBE SPRINGS
HIDDEN GOLD

One of the most interesting desert expeditions is to an area of the Providence Mountains called Globe Springs near the small town of Kelso. Few people in the Kelso-Cima Dome vicinity even know that the spring still exists.

There are two ways of reaching this spring, providing either road is still there. One route reaches over a high chain of cliffs; the other snakes through the narrow walls of a deep canyon. The cliff route is difficult and the canyon nearly impassable. Either way takes several hours of hair-raising four-wheel driving.

In many parts of the Globe Springs region the surfaces of the cliffs and hills are composed of rich minerals and oresdull, burnished galena and beckoning fool's gold. Deep shafts and tunnels mark endeavors of long-departed miners. A cave in the Providence Mountains is said to date back to prehistoric man and more recent visitors. There are also tales of loot from Wells Fargo robberies being hidden there and of gold coins Spanish explorers had cached away in the depths of the cave.

Following a torn, stained and almost unreadable old map, we made our way into the mountains looking for two distinct landmarks. The first was a volcanic mass of rock forming a bluff and secondly, a huge, twisted dead conifer tree pointing its grotesque limbs toward the cave entrance. After several hours of searching we sighted the tree and within 200 yards we spotted the entrance to the cave. We made our way up the steep slope and arrived at an opening 15 feet high and 20 feet wide.

Within the mouth the reddish rock slides were pitted with holes, probably used as shelves by whoever had lived there. Large spikes, driven into the walls, likely served to hang lanterns, clothing and gear.

Near the crude fireplace at the back of the cave we found a broken earthen pot and a piece of a silver belt buckle, heavily engraved with plumed birds. We searched in vain for other relics, finding only a few scraps of old rusty iron.

Across the narrow valley we saw what appeared at first to be a large shadow on a hillside. Looking through binoculars, it proved to be the mouth of a large cave, an opening so indistinct there was the possibility that the cave would be unexplored. Climbing down to the valley floor, we lost sight of this second cave, so decided to climb to where we thought it might be. After more than an hour of unsuccessful searching, we decided to retreat to our first position and re-sight this cave's location by landmarks. We trudged back only to find sundown had changed the mountain into a glowing forest of gold. The unexplored cave had disappeared and we would have to wait to spot it again.

While in the midst of finding the deep canyon, exploring the first cave and drinking from the icy spring, it was not difficult to imagine ourselves living a hundred years earlier. As explorers had seen the Globe Springs region a century before, so had we seen it, as so little of the landscape has changed. Nature's processes are slow and very few people have ever found their way here to disturb the area's pristine condition.

Directions: Drive north on I-15 for 40 north of Baker to the Cima Road exit. Turn right for 18 miles to Cima, then continue for 15 miles to Globe Canyon, 4 miles north of Kelso. At the base of the mountains to your left are a myriad of canyons with springs and trails.

Globe Springs PHOTO: LESLIE PAYNE

From Las Vegas, drive south on I-15 for 66 miles to the Cima Road exit. 4WD recommended.

Map: AAA San Bernardino County, DeLorme's Southern California Atlas & Gazetteer

High in the Providence Mountains PHOTO: WYNNE BENTI

BLACK CANYON, BONANZA KING MINE, FOSHAY PASS, KELSO & THE PROVIDENCE MOUNTAINS

Black Canyon Road is definitely the gateway to adventure. From the first mile to the last, there exists a myriad of trails to be followed, mountains to climb and scenery to enjoy and photograph. Campgrounds at Mid-Hills and Hole-in-the-Wall make ideal headquarters from which to explore. It would be virtually impossible to tell of all the sites to visit, and besides, it's more fun to seek them out by yourself. I'll just touch on my favorites.

Granite Well is a lovely sport for a picnic, just 1.5 miles off Black Canyon Road. But Wildhorse Canyon Road is the ultimate in seclusion as it stretches in an easterly direction over 12 miles, deep into the heart of the towering Providence Mountains. The next old road to follow leads east to Bonanza King Mine, the Silver King Mine and the crumbled ruins of Providence. A few miles east of these pockmarked hills are Bear Claw Well and Domingo Spring. All are but a few, short bumpy miles off Black Canyon Road.

If you want a break from driving, visit Mitchell Cavern State Park. The caverns are some of the finest I've seen, always a cool 56 degrees inside, a welcome stop on a warm day.

Next on the agenda is the hair-raising trip over Foshay Pass. This rutted, high-climbing trail is at the best in spring and summer months. Winter snows make it next to impossible to follow. Foshay Pass was the scene of tremendous mining activity during the years of World War II, when iron ore was discovered.

Kelso Depot   PHOTO: WYNNE BENTI

Henry J. Kaiser built the now defunct Vulcan Mine about midway through the narrow pass. Today the abandoned mine gives one an eerie feeling. The cavernous pit seems to extend to Hades, and, as strange as it sounds, there are few persons who visit this remote derelict mine that don't feel the uneasiness and skin-prickling sensation. I, for one, would rather cut a wide path around this particular place.

Shortly before coming to the Vulcan Mine, there are three springs—Coletta Spring, Blind Spring and Foshay Spring. Near the summit of the pass, which is over 4,375 feet, is Summit Spring, at about the 4,100 foot level. Rising northward at an altitude of 7,000 feet above sea level is impressive Mt. Edgar.

The Providence Mountains' most striking feature is apparent as one descends Foshay Pass into the railroad town of Kelso. A series of great west-facing cliffs loom skyward. These cliffs, supported by massive Mississippian limestone, are even more impressive from the railroad station platform at Kelso. There are sharp ridges that rise like a buttress to meet the base of the great cliffs. The most prominent of these ridges borders on Cornfield Springs Canyon, where they reach an altitude of 4,000 feet.

The nine mile trip through Foshay Pass is one that any adventure-seeker will long remember.

Directions: Take I-15 26.2 miles north of Baker, turning south on the Cima off-ramp for 17.3 miles to the town of Cima. Continuing south for 4.4 miles to Cedar Canyon Road. Drive east 4.5 miles to Black Canyon, turning south, for 8.3 miles to Hole-in-the-Wall Campground and Desert Info Station. Continue another 8.9 miles to the five-way intersection with the Essex-Providence Park Road. Turn right on the paved road for 6 miles to the state park. For Foshay Pass, head west (4WD recommended) over the rough pass for 6 miles to the Vulcan Mine and pavement. Kelso is 9 miles northwest.

Alternate: Take I-15 to Barstow, I-40 to Ludlow, then 28.2 miles to the Essex-Providence off-ramp. The five-way intersection lies 9.2 miles to the northwest. Follow above directions for Providence and Foshay Pass. Turn north for Black Canyon, and Cima. 4WD suggested for the canyon.

Map: AAA San Bernardino County, DeLorme's Southern California Atlas & Gazetteer

Heading from Kelso to Cima on the Kelso-Cima Road PHOTO: WYNNE BENTI

TOLTEC MINE
ANCIENT MINERS
—⊕—

I once befriended an old-timer on a California desert trail. He told me a story which inspired several trips to the old Toltec Mine in the Shadow Mountains of northeastern San Bernardino County. He recounted tales of turquoise, of prehistoric miners who, many centuries ago, came into the desert in search of precious stones. They made friends with the natives and began to work many mines. For centuries great quantities of the beautiful blue stone were taken from the area annually and carried south to their distant country.

The old-timer's story also suggested that these newcomers possessed many arts unknown in the region and passed on their knowledge to the ancestor of the Mojave nation. But a powerful neighboring tribe distrusted the newcomers and resolved on a war of extermination. After a long conflict most of the strangers were slain and the mines abandoned until some of the old workings were rediscovered in the late 1800s.

An old prospector had observed a small hill where the float rock was seamed and stained with blue. Digging down a few feet, he found a vein of turquoise—a white talcose material inclosing nodules and small masses of the mineral. At a depth of twenty feet he found fine gem color and two early stone hammers.

At the first opportunity we headed for the Shadow Mountains. From Las Vegas we headed west, pausing at the Halloran Springs Service Station to check the speedometer. Just a few hundred feet west of the station we took a trail to the right towards some hills, through an area strewn with basalt blocks. Approaching them we came on an old blacktop road at the power line. It served us for only a short distance before we turned left onto another desert trail.

Reaching Halloran Springs, it is easy to visualize an age when prehistoric miners carried on their labors. Today the spring has been piped into a tank which furnishes water for stock. At the fork beyond the spring we turned left and dropped down a sandy slope past a large outcropping of brown stone and continued on across a wash. Climbing the ridge to the north, we followed an old burro trail which undulates sharply and transverses four ridges and three canyons. At the second ridge we found an old glory hole near the rugged reddish-brown outcrop of rock, which the local people call the glass mountain.

Beyond the immediate terrain a breath-taking panorama unfolds in the clear air. The powerline crossing the northern tip of Silver Dry Lake is visible, as is a dry lake farther north, the Soda Mountains, the Avawatz Range and the bright white workings of a distant talc quarry.

When the first signs of the ancient people who worked the Toltec Mine site were discovered in 1897, there were still many open pits there. These original quarry workings were not large, but were extensive in number. Until the recent large dumps crept westward, there was still one of the old pits not more than a hundred feet from the entrance of the old Toltec Mine, but modern man and erosion have now erased all vestiges of their existence.

Toltec Mine area   PHOTO: LESLIE PAYNE

Directions: New modern roads have now changed the approach. Take I-15 north from Baker for 13 miles to Halloran Springs exit. Follow the road north for 6 miles to a microwave station junction. Continue west for 4 miles to the site.

Alternate: Cross I-15 to Halloran Springs. Turn left on a dirt road for 4 miles, north across a sandy wash for 2 miles to the various mine sites. 4WD recommended for this trip.

From Las Vegas, take I-15 south to the Halloran Springs off-ramp, 71 miles. Turn right and follow above directions.

Map: AAA San Bernardino County, DeLorme's Southern California Atlas & Gazetteer

Third-class route to the summit of Clark Mountain   PHOTO: WYNNE BENTI

CLARK MOUNTAIN
AZTEC WORKINGS IN THE MOJAVE

Massive Clark Mountain rises precipitously from the desert floor and is crowned with a forest of dwarf conifers. Limestone mountains almost always harbor peculiar species of plant and animals, as well as interesting minerals, and Clark Mountain is no exception. In this case, minerals are what first called attention to this rugged peak.

On March 18, 1898, the San Francisco Call carried a short article about an expedition that had ventured into a remote canyon and found exterior mines of precious turquoise stones of the highest quality. Here, also, they were surprised to see a series of intricate petroglyphs, numbering in the tens of thousands, extending for more than twenty miles around the mines.

Twenty or more caves dotted the canyon wall below. It is believed that prehistoric mine workers once lived in these caves as they worked the mines. The San Francisco Call article claimed that bits of pottery, stone implements and tools were abundant as well. Expedition reports stated that these were indeed the turquoise mines from which the great Aztec chief, Montezuma, secured his sacred blue stones so important to his now extinct culture. This is a most interesting yarn, however it conflicts with authentic historic reports.

About the turn of the century, an old prospector had been given probable directions by someone who claimed to have seen the old diggings. It seemed that when the sun reached a certain position in the sky, it would cast a triangular shadow at the base of Clark Mountain. In the southernmost point of the triangle, a small canyon opened up, revealing strange Indian symbols. This area was black with volcanic rock and eerie in all aspects.

When this prospector reached a waterhole that for years had been an unfailing source of water, he found it dry. He gazed in horror at the once verdant spot. Scarcely a gulp of water remained in his canteen and twenty miles or more of searing desert lay between him and the next spring. Could he possibly last until he reached his destination? Many others had failed. Making his way through rock-strewn sands, the old man carefully hoarded his meager water supply. Intense heat combined with the driest climate in existence was quickly sapping the moisture from his body.

The desert plays strange tricks on one's perceptions. A twenty-mile distance can appear as one. Other times, one mile can appear as twenty. Stumbling, half crawling, finally the old man could go no farther. Fear no longer gripped his heart, for the fear had faded within the shadow of the legendary treasure mountain. Many months passed before his skeleton was discovered and many more years have passed since his story was first told. Clark Mountain still guards this prospector's secret. Try your luck. Hopefully you will be more fortunate than that old man.

Directions: Take I-15 north for 35 miles from Baker to Mountain Pass. Turn north and follow an access road 5.6 miles to a dirt road turning right. It is 7.5 miles to Clark Mountain.

From Las Vegas take I-15 south for 60 miles to Mountain Pass and exit.
Map: AAA San Bernardino County, DeLorme's Southern California Atlas & Gazetteer

SEARCHLIGHT TO THE NEW YORK MOUNTAINS
BOOM AND BUST

—✳—

Nature's forces are always changing the face of our earth. Free-flowing springs dry up while new ones slowly bubble to the surface. Land builds up and erodes away, streams change course and volcanoes erupt into new mountains or large, deep craters. Humankind also impacts on the earth's terrain, but perhaps not so permanently. Prospectors find precious ores in the hard-crusted earth and proceed to erect a mine shaft frame, shelter, a mill and perhaps even a whole new town. The vein drifts; men leave and in time the desert erases almost every footprint left by those intruders.

At one time, Searchlight reportedly attracted more than 8,000 people looking for that elusive strike, but through the years the hustle and bustle has calmed down to a population of just over 600. Although little remains of the Searchlight of 1907, it is still a gateway to a desert wilderness beyond compare.

A mile-and-a-half southwest of Searchlight is a dirt road that winds through twenty long miles of adventure and history. Scenery along this route is varied to an extreme; broad expanses of wasteland, high jagged mountain peaks, deep arroyos and sand-swept hummocks covered with mesquite. Strangely enough, dry as it appears, the region is dotted with springs. Just over the Nevada-California border in the New York Mountains, are five active springs—Indian, Talc, Malpais, Stagecoach and Dove Springs. All are tiny oases in this vast and lonely desert.

The site of Barnwell PHOTO: LESLIE PAYNE

In the late 1880s when mining was in full swing, these springs were hubs of activity because, although the price of gold was at an all-time high, the value of clear water was even higher. The long-gone mining camps of Hart, in the Castle Mountains, and Barnwell in the New York Mountains, were dependent upon these springs, not only to sustain life for the miners and their families, but for the processing of their ores as well.

Gold producing veins in these booming camps were copper-stained quartz in fissures of andesite, or bird's-eye porphry. Barnwell was also an agricultural center from 1905 to 1907, growing enough fresh produce to supply several other mining camps in this region. Now Hart and Barnwell are ghosts, clad in silvery, weathered wood, crumbling stone and rutted empty streets leading nowhere. The hills around these two towns are pocketed with mine tunnels, so caution should be observed upon approach. Slag piles below each hole glitter with colorful ore. Brilliant blue azurite, bright green malachite and smoky quartz are among the more common stones.

Traveling in any direction from either of these two towns can be a most rewarding experience. The springs, the stark and rugged peaks and sheer serenity of the region, are the natural ingredients for an interesting trip.

Directions: Drive 40 miles north of Baker on I-15 to the Nipton exit. Head east on the Nipton Road for 3.5 miles to the Ivanpah Road. Continue past Ivanpah 7 miles to Barnwell. For Hart, turn left from Barnwell, on the Hart Mine Road for 5 miles, then right for 4 miles to the site of Hart.

From Las Vegas, take US-95 for 54 miles to Searchlight. Jog west for 1.1 miles, south for 0.7 miles, then southwest on Hart Road for 16.6 miles to a junction. Hart lies four miles to the right; Barnwell, 5 miles ahead.

Map: AAA San Bernardino County, DeLorme's Southern California Atlas & Gazetteer

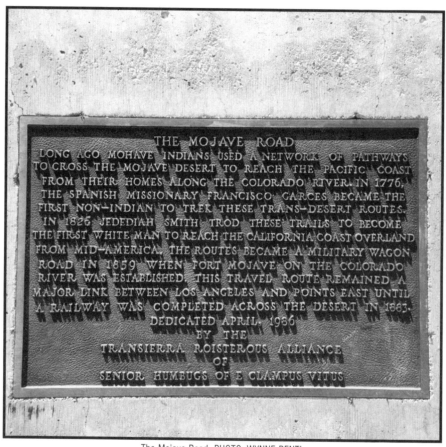

The Mojave Road PHOTO: WYNNE BENTI

TALKING MOUNTAIN
PASS BY AT A SAFE DISTANCE
—✳—

Carved upon the rocky surfaces of this massive stone hill, are the figures of animals, men and symbols—each executed with truly remarkable skill, considering the crude implements used to incise the lines into a medium much harder than glass. These petroglyphs represent a phase of prehistoric art that is incredibly significant. Like the murals on the tombs of the Pharaohs, scenes of hunting, battles and mysterious rituals are etched in stone, a valuable source of material for those who would study these ancient writings.

In one area the scheme is of horizontal rows of triangular ornaments fringed at top and bottom. Some resemble rows of pipes or horns, while others depict men in extravagant headdresses. Among the ensemble of drawings, animals seem to be in the majority. There are mountain sheep, deer and antelope. Some are shown standing, others running. A whimsical touch is now and then shown by the artists, as many of the quadrupeds have pot bellies, swayed backs and distorted heads. One may roam for hours around this massive monolithic outcropping and see that every available square foot of the smooth patina-coated stone is covered with drawings.

Nearby is a deep, slanted tank-like depression which has been given the name of Indian Well. When we visited here, the water was low and bordered on stagnation, but still offered enough life-giving fluids for the small desert creatures that make their way here. The country around Indian Hill is lovely—high enough to be verdant in spring, dotted with yucca trees, desert willows and seasonal wildflowers. It is a curious blend of hillsides and plains.

Ancient legend suggest that there was once a great mountain near Indian Hill, feared by the ancestors of the Paiute and Shoshone. They called it Talking Mountain and would travel miles out of their way to avoid passing close to its flanks. One day, according to the legend, Talking Mountain grew so angry that it roared and hurled boulders far into the air, so far that the projectiles became invisible. When the smoke and the dust cleared away from the mountain's terrible outburst, all that remained was the strange monolith we now call Indian Hill.

Directions: Drive 40 miles north of Baker on I-15 to the Nipton exit and go east on the Nipton Road for 3.5 miles to the Ivanpah Road. Continue past Ivanpah toward Goffs for 13.7 miles. Turn left for 2.2 miles. The road then splits. The right fork goes for 1.6 miles; the left fork goes for two miles. Indian Hill lies in the middle of the two forks.

From Las Vegas, take I-15 south for 54 miles to the Nipton turnoff and follow the directions above.

Map: AAA San Bernardino County, DeLorme's Southern California Atlas & Gazetteer

B R I S T O L   D R Y   L A K E
CAMBRIAN CREATURES

Hundreds of years ago, Bristol Dry Lake was part of an ancient Cambrian sea filled with a variety of primitive animal forms, such as the trilobites from the Paleozoic Era. These small creatures had been a dominant form of life on earth for millions of years and still had millions of years to go. But then, as the sea built up and the climate changed and the land rose and sank, and lifted again, the world moved into the age of fishes and the trilobites faded away to become part of the geologic record.

Today there is a trilobite graveyard in the Marble Mountains at the northeastern edge of the Bristol sink. From below Sheephead Pass, twenty-five air-miles away, one can see the tip of the Marbles where the upturned, faulted Cambrian formations are spectacularly displayed. Reaching Amboy, you turn east and follow the road to Chambless, then angle south on the surfaced road to Cadiz Station on the railroad. The fossil beds lie about two miles northwest of Cadiz at an old marble quarry. It is possible, with a four-wheel-drive, to follow the old marble quarry road to the base of the Cambrian cliffs in which these fossils are found.

There are pieces of red-spotted limestone, in which the red circles and ovals have been identified as algae. The trail divides at the base of the spectacular banded cliffs; the left branch slants up and around to the little bay of trilobites, the right one leading to the main quarry, which appears to have been untouched for some time. A wooden boom, part of the tackle used to hoist the fifteen and twenty-ton marble blocks, still stands, tall enough to mark the canyon for several miles.

This marble was discovered in 1937 and mined until 1939. About 2,000 feet of highly colored Calevanto marble was cut from this quarry and used in such buildings as the Gardena and Oxnard post offices, as well as the custom house in San Francisco.

It is a short hike to the trilobite shales, a Lower Cambrian formation about forty feet thick, with quartzite and calcareous layers inter-bedded. Trilobite and brachiopod remains are abundant, but do not take them out of the rock. Leave them for others to enjoy.

We have never found an entire adult trilobite. Most of their bones were the head shields with spines. We have seen a thorax with appendages and the little dots, which are said to be trilobite eggs, as well as tiny segmented moults of the small fry. In most trilobite deposits, only the dorsal shield, the thick upper portion of the external skeleton, normally survives, and it often splits between the head shield and the fragile thorax.

If you climb to the top of the highest tilted edge, you'll discover an awesome view of the upthrust, broken and eroded sediments which once had been a level sea bed. Wonderful, too, is the view across Bristol Dry Lake, which usually does not look dry, but drowned in shimmering, silvery water mirages. The effect is even more amazing driving across the Dry Lake, between Amboy and Sheephole Pass. Looking back across the lake at the tip of the Marbles, the bases of the mountains will seem to be under water and the peaks themselves waver and fade in the rolling heat waves. It is a realm where time appears to have stopped.

Directions: Take I-15 north to Barstow, then right on I-40 to Ludlow. Again turning right, follow National Trails Highway (old Route 66) for 28.3 miles to Amboy. Bristol Dry Lake is just south of Amboy.

From Las Vegas, take US-95 south to near Needles. Take a bypass to I-40, 2 miles north of Needles. Drive west on I-40 for 66 miles to the Amboy cut-off (Kelbaker Road) to National Trails Highway, traveling 11 miles. Amboy is now 6 miles to the west.

Map: AAA San Bernardino County, DeLorme's Southern California Atlas & Gazetteer

Fort Piute area PHOTO: LESLIE PAYNE

FORT PIUTE
WRITINGS OF THE ANCIENTS
— ✳ —

The crumbling ruins of Fort Piute on the Old Government Road are all that remain of this once important but short-lived army camp. It was in 1867 that orders were sent to establish an outpost in the Mohave Desert for the protection of numerous wagon trains and for the convenience of mail carriers.

The first Piute establishment was a simple corral built from local materials—willows from the creek bed and rawhide to secure the fence. Next came two stone houses built from native rock, so abundant in the area. One of the structures housed the soldiers; the other was used as a general purpose room—kitchen, storage and perhaps even an arsenal. In just over six months the fort or outpost was abandoned and soon the elements returned the site back to its original primitive state. Today, one can still explore the stone foundations that now house only desert creatures. The corral may also be found with a little diligent searching.

Long before the United States Army established Fort Piute, prehistoric nomads inhabited the area. Instead of leaving behind foundations and relics, they left a vast array of petroglyphs—writings intricately pecked into the smooth desert-varnished rocks. Some say petroglyphs are nonsensical doodling, but in recent years, many experts such as cryptographer, Lavan Martineau, have shed new light on the rock writings. Martineau's widely acclaimed book, THE ROCKS BEGIN TO SPEAK, illustrates the significance of these fascinating petroglyphs left behind by ancient people.

Not only is the Fort Piute area interesting for its historical aspect and Native American culture; it is a site of tremendous beauty. Piute Creek, a reliable water source, is a refreshing, restful spot in the desert. Piute Spring is also nearby. The spring is still one of the most beautiful primitive and undisturbed areas left in the Mojave Desert.

The early Chemehuevi Indians left many foot paths around Piute Valley. These faint trails are great to hike. Follow one up Piute Hill. It is a strenuous climb but worth it when you reach the summit. Piute Valley stretches out before you with conical-shaped Jed Smith Butte (or Lookout Mountain) guarding the entrance to the Fort Piute region. In the distance one can discern the remains of the old Irwin Ranch and the picturesque washes draining into the valley.

Directions: From Las Vegas, go south toward Searchlight on US-95. At 22.9 miles past Searchlight, turn southwest on a dirt road. Go 8.2 miles to the ruins of Fort Piute. [4WD]

Map: AAA San Bernardino County, DeLorme's Southern California Atlas & Gazetteer

FORT MOHAVE
SAFE PASSAGE ACROSS THE COLORADO
—⊕—

It is said that being ordered to Fort Mohave in the 1860s was like being banished to hell. The climate was unbearable—over 120 degrees in the summer and well below freezing in the winter. When river traffic was working, supplies came up the Colorado. Captain George Johnson, who first piloted a steamboat up the river, wrote: "We left Fort Yuma December 20, 1857... and reached the head of navigation, it being seventy-four miles above Fort Mohave, the point where Lieutenant Beale crossed the Colorado."

But sandbars, low water and lack of profitable traffic often grounded the little steamer. When the steamer wasn't running, the only option was traveling over the desert, land of little or no rain. The roads were always difficult, even impassable at times. There was no fresh food, for even when wagon trains arrived from the east, it took months to traverse the desert's rugged land. Mail came infrequently and cabin fever—not to mention disease, took its toll on the men stationed there. Morale was low. Violence, murder, madness and death by misadventure were commonplace.

Fort Mohave was originally called "Beale's Crossing," after Lieutenant Edward Beale, who made an initial survey of the region in 1857. It soon became a major crossing on the Colorado River for settlers travelling west to the California gold fields. A small fort was set up by Lieutenant Colonel William Hoffman, who called it "Camp Colorado." By April of 1859, however, Major Lewis Armistead took over command and changed the name to Fort Mohave. But after less than two years the fort was abandoned.

Out and about in the East Mojave. PHOTO: LESLIE PAYNE

With the advent of the Civil War, approximately half of the soldiers, who were Southerners, deserted and returned to fight alongside their Confederate brothers. The fort was reinstated in 1863, with fresh loyal troops from California.

In 1890, Fort Mohave was turned over to the Department of the Interior, to be used as an Indian school. The school served Indians in the region until its closing in 1932, when the land became part of the Fort Mohave Indian Reservation. Today the remains of Fort Mohave is about eight miles south of Bullhead City on the Arizona side of the Colorado River, then two miles west overlooking the river. All that remains are stone foundations peppered with brush and sand, empty ditches and sidewalks which generally go unnoticed by passing motorists.

These crumbling ruins tell many stories about the struggles of those people who lived and died on this small uplift of land. I have explored the area and each time I have been rewarded with a remnant of the past: a brass uniform button, several glass trade beads, a sliver of purpled glass—a bit of history in each discovery. I have searched for a clue as to where the barracks once were or the hospital or the officers' quarters. At the river's edge there is evidence of the location of the ferry that transported such well-known historical figures as Jedediah Strong Smith and Edward Beale, with his caravans of camels and men.

The primitive ferry was quite simple, but remarkably efficient: a small flat scow, sometimes constructed of old wagon beds. A rope-cable was tightly stretched directly across the stream. Two pulleys were hooked over the cable, and a short line tied to each end of the scow. The trailing line was lengthened, setting the scow at an angle, and the flow of the stream forced the craft ahead. It did not work too well on a slow stream, but on the surging Colorado, it was quickly swept across the river. In times of low water, local Native Americans used poles and oars to prod it along. Thus the ferry crossed endlessly from shore to shore, as impatient travelers awaited their turn.

The site is quiet now. Sometimes the river is calm and green and at other times it boils red mud. The black volcanic mountains are clearly defined in the crisp air and blending desert light and shadows are beautiful. Fort Mohave may lie in rubble, but its ghosts are still here.

Directions: Take I-15 to Barstow, then right on I-40 to Needles. Cross the Colorado River, then north on Mohave Valley Road (AZ-95), for about ten miles to a junction with a good gravel road. This leads west for a mile to the site of fort near the river's bank.

From Las Vegas, take US-95 south to the Bullhead City turnoff (NV-163). From Bullhead City turn south for 10.6 miles to the exit to the Fort Mohave site.

Map: AAA San Bernardino County, DeLorme's Southern California Atlas & Gazetteer

TURTLE MOUNTAINS
WATER IS GOLD

Rugged, forbidding and practically waterless, the Turtle Range is one of the most impressive sights in the Mojave Desert. Legends about the range date back to the 1860s, when La Paz, in the Arizona Territory, now completely obliterated, was the largest settlement on the Colorado River.

Many decades ago, Mohave Indians appeared at stores with quantities of gold dust which they exchanged for goods. Prospectors by the score made every effort to trail the elusive Indians to their secret cache. For the most part their efforts were in vain, but one fact seems established beyond dispute—the Indians were mining their placer gold in a rugged mountain range, some twenty-six miles west of the Colorado. But the classic tales of the Turtle Mountains are those of two lost mines, the Lost Arch and the Lost Tub.

About ninety years ago, two prospectors entered the Turtle Range with one pack animal and a two-day supply of water. Arriving at their destination, they were faced with the necessity of finding more water immediately. They split up—one entered a narrow valley, the other entered a gorge in hope of locating a spring or water cache. Neither was successful, but the partner who had explored the canyon returned with exciting news. Nor far from the head of the gorge, he found a natural bridge of stone spanning the dry watercourse. Pausing to rest in the shade of the arch, he idly scratched the sand with his boot. Instantly he noticed

Migrating tarantula. PHOTO: WYNNE BENTI

the sand was unusually heavy. A closer look revealed the reason—
it contained gold dust!

The prospectors found wealth beyond their wildest dreams, but their canteens were stone dry. The only sure water source was the Colorado River. They turned eastward across the sweltering desert. After great hardship they arrived at the river in extremely poor condition. One of the men died from exposure, while the other lived to show his gold to others.

Only the notorious lack of water in the Turtle Mountains held back a major gold rush. Occasionally some dare devil prospector would stake his life on an attempt to find the source of that rich placer, the Lost Arch. No records exist to show the number of men who tried and returned empty-handed, or how many never came back at all.

About 70 years ago, another two men traveled in a wagon loaded with barrels of water. Besides the conventional equipment for washing gold dust, they carried a tub to catch the water for reuse. When they finally succeeded in sinking their picks into pay dirt, only a few gallons remained. In a short time $12,000 in coarse gold was stored away in canvas bags, while an undetermined amount remained in the muck on the bottom of the tub. With barely enough drinking water left, they cached the tub in a small cave and returned home.

For some reason, the two men were never able to go back. In years that followed, scores of other seekers trekked through the rugged region searching for a narrow sandy wash in a deep gorge with a small cave containing a tub. So far as is known, rediscovery has never been made, but the search gave birth to a sage of hidden treasure... the Lost Tub.

The Turtle Mountains are about 35 miles long and 17 miles wide, covering an area of 600 square miles of very primitive country. It is probable that rich ore lies in abundance, but the trick is to find it.

Directions: Take I-15 to Barstow, then right on I-40 toward Needles. Turn south on US-95 past Lake Havasu turnoff to Vidal Junction, 47 miles. Turn west for 19 miles to Rice, then head north to Turtle Mountains. [4WD]. From Las Vegas take US-95 south 93 miles to Needles and follow above directions.

Alternate: Take I-10 toward Palm Springs, then north on CA-62 to Twenty-nine Palms. Continue on CA-92 for 59 miles to Rice.

Map: AAA San Bernardino County, DeLorme's Southern California Atlas & Gazetteer

On the summit of Turtle Mountain. PHOTO: WYNNE BENTI

TO THE TOP OF

TURTLE MOUNTAIN

BY ANDY ZDON

— ⊕ —

TURTLE MOUNTAIN (4,313 FT; 1,310+ M)

Turtle Mountain's excellent view of the Mopah Peaks area is certainly worth the long, rough approach route. To the southwest is "Horn Peak" (3,864 ft), unnamed on the topo, that can be climbed from the same road end as Turtle.

Maps: Mopah Peaks and Horn Spring (CA) 7.5-minute (1:24,000) scale topographic maps; Parker 1:100,000 scale metric topographic map; Automobile Club of Southern California (AAA) San Bernardino County map

Best Time to Climb: November through April

Approach: From Twentynine Palms, California on State Highway 62, drive 83 miles east on Highway 62 to a dirt road 0.7 miles east of milepost 117 (beyond a railroad crossing). This turnoff is also 8.1 miles west of Vidal Junction. Follow this dirt road 0.2 miles crossing the Metropolitan Water District Aqueduct then turn left on a dirt road 1.8 miles to a junction. If driving into the area at night, it is recommended that you stop and camp here for the evening. The rest of the road is nearly impossible to follow at night, and four-wheel drive is required from this point on. Head northwest, continuing 5.2 miles to a faint road to the right. Turn southeast onto this road and follow it 0.3 miles into a wash. Follow the road through the wash 0.1 miles where it exits the east edge of the wash and heads north. Continue another 4.7 miles, bearing left at a fork and driving another 0.5 miles. Park just before the road enters a sandy wash at 2,330 feet.

Route: Hike generally northwest along the wash 1.3 miles to a broad low saddle. Turtle Mountain, and much of the northern peaks of the Turtle Mountains will come into view here. Head generally west-northwest, gradually gaining elevation and crossing numerous washes en route until east of the peak. Head west up Turtle's east ridge to a point just south of the summit, then north a short distance to the summit. The views of Umpah and Mopah from the route, will inspire the occasional, well-earned rest stop. Anticipate seven miles round-trip with 2,100 feet of elevation gain.

"Rice" looks much bigger on the map than it is in reality. Driving by its one windowless and weatherworn bungalow I realized how remote an area this was. Not far from Rice, we left the highway, headed for the

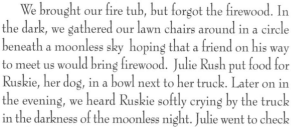

Turtle Mountains deep in the Mojave Desert. Soon, the landscape changed from the classic sprawling creosote flats of the Mojave to a mass of fantastic buttes and mesas, both ethereal and surreal.

We brought our fire tub, but forgot the firewood. In the dark, we gathered our lawn chairs around in a circle beneath a moonless sky hoping that a friend on his way to meet us would bring firewood. Julie Rush put food for Ruskie, her dog, in a bowl next to her truck. Later on in the evening, we heard Ruskie softly crying by the truck in the darkness of the moonless night. Julie went to check on him, but none of us noticed that his food bowl had vanished.

The next morning we drove closer to the trailhead. About a half mile down the road in the middle of the wash, Julie found Ruskie's dish. The bowl was empty, but the coyote left his signature: several teeth marks in the plastic. — *Wynne Benti*

Julie and Ruskie on Turtle Mountain. PHOTO: WYNNE BENTI

WHIPPLE MOUNTAINS
OLDEST ROCKS
—⊕—

The Whipple Mountains are a low desert range lying northeast of Vidal Junction, California on a crossroad between Blythe and Needles on US-95. The mountains stretch east and west, bounded by Lake Havasu's water on the east and on the west by US-95 that cuts through a wide alluvial valley separating the Whipple Mountains from the Turtle Range.

This region, most lavishly decorated with collectable minerals, is still relatively untouched by humankind. Here and there are a few glory holes abandoned when miners gave up their search for precious ores. Some mines with remains of rather extensive work are still visible, but for the most part, the mountains and land are as they have been for centuries.

From the highway the Whipples are a striking range. Seen up close they are among the most beautiful mountains in the Mojave. Much of their spectacular scenery is due to their make-up, a jumbled composition of some of the world's oldest rocks—pre-Cambrian granites, schists and quartzites with the colorful volcanics of Tertiary times. Their beauty is augmented by heavy vegetation—ironwood, palo verde and smoke trees, more reminiscent of the Colorado Desert than of the Mojave.

As the road swings around the southern slopes of the mountains toward the Colorado River, a lean column of dark volcanic rock comes into sight in the northeast. This is famed Monument Peak, a landmark since the beginnings of desert habitation. Many of the narrow canyons in the Whipple Mountains have sandy floors

Whipple Mountains. PHOTO: WYNNE BENTI

liberally scattered with chalcedony roses, some the size of a dime, others as large as an average human hand. Their colors range from white to creamy brown and orange to pale pink. Chalcedony is a form of quarts, the commonest of minerals, yet there is nothing common about these beautiful translucent gemstones.

Numerous old roads lead into the foothills where jasper and agate can be found in colors of red, yellow, gold, brown and even sometimes a lovely greenish shade. There is also evidence of early Indians who worked these fields, searching for suitable material for arrowheads and spear points. The chippings from their labors indicate they selected their stones with an eye for beauty, as well as practicality. It is surprising how many different colors can be found in just a handful of these smooth flakes.

Directions: Take I-15 to Barstow, then turn right on I-40 for 144 miles to Needles. Turn right on US-95, past Lake Havasu turnoff, for 50 miles, to Vidal Junction. The Whipple Mountains lie east and north from here. They may be reached by taking the aqueduct maintenance road, about one mile north of Vidal Junction. From this road, numerous routes (4WD or walking) lead into the foothills, oftentimes to old mine sites. From Las Vegas take US-95 south for 93 miles to Needles. From there, follow the above directions.

Map: AAA San Bernardino County, DeLorme's Southern California Atlas & Gazetteer

Important Addresses and Phone Numbers

Bureau of Land Management,
Barstow Field Office
2601 Barstow Road
Barstow, California 92311
Phone (760)252-6000
Fax (760)252-6099
Web Site - www.ca.blm.gov/barstow

Bureau of Land Management,
El Centro Field Office
1661 S. 4th Street
El Centro, California 92243
Phone (760)337-4400
Web Site - www.ca.blm.gov/elcentro

Bureau of Land Management,
Las Vegas Field Office
4765 W. Vegas Drive
Las Vegas, Nevada 89108-2135
Phone (702)647-5000
Fax (702)647-5023
Web Site - www.nv.blm.gov/vegas

Bureau of Land Management,
Needles Field Office
101 W. Spikes Road
Needles, California 92363
Phone (760)326-7000
Fax (760)326-7099
Web Site - www.ca.blm.gov/needles

Bureau of Land Management,
Palm Springs South Coast Field Office
690 Garnet Avenue, P.O. Box 1260
Palm Springs, California 92258
Phone (760)251-4800
Fax (760)251-4899
Web Site - www.ca.blm.gov/palmsprings

Bureau of Land Management,
Ridgecrest Field Office
300 S. Richmond Road
Ridgecrest, California 93555
Phone (760)384-5400
Fax (760)384-5499
Web Site - www.ca.blm.gov/ridgecrest

Bureau of Land Management,
California Desert District Office
6221 Box Springs Boulevard
Riverside, California 92507
Phone (909)697-5200
Fax (909)697-5299
Web Site - www.ca.blm.gov/cdd

Mojave National Preserve
222 E. Main Street, Suite 202
Barstow, California 92311
Phone (760)255-8801
Web Site - www.nps.gov/moja/index.htm

Mojave National Preserve
Baker Information Center
75157 Baker Boulevard, P.O. Box 241
Baker, California 92309
Phone (760)733-4040
Web Site - www.nps.gov/moja/index.htm

Mojave National Preserve
Needles Information Center
707 W. Broadway
Needles, California 92363
Phone (760)326-6322

Providence Mountains
State Recreation Area
Essex, California
Phone (760)928-2586
Web Site - www.parks.ca.gov/
Click on "Find a Park"

Red Rock Canyon National Conservation Area
HCR 33, Box 5500
Las Vegas, Nevada 89124
Phone (702)363-1921
Web Site - www.redrockcanyon.blm.gov

San Bernardino National Forest-
San Jacinto Ranger District
P.O. Box 518
Idyllwild, California 92549
Phone (909)659-2117
WebSite - www.fs.fed.us/r5/sanbernardino

Desert Essentials

Basics for the car
- Road map (AAA maps or DeLorme Atlas & Gazetteer maps)
- Cell phone (limited or no reception in may desert areas)
- Water (six to eight gallons minimum, separate containers, for two people on one waterless weekend)
- Tire jack, spare tire, lug wrench, tool kit, battery jumper cables, roll of duct tape, tow-rope
- Can of puncture seal (for emergency flats when the spare has been used)
- Cooler (with fruit juices, soda, preferably with sugar, sports drink like Gatorade)
- 2 two to three foot long two by four boards (for tires that get stuck in sand)
- Small collapsible shovel

Basics for the overnight car camp:
- Water (extra containers), food
- Camp stove, cooking utensils
- Roll-away camp table, lawn chairs
- Ground cloth
- Sleeping bags (wrap cooler during the day, in the car, to insulate from sun)
- Sleeping pads
- Firewood, metal tub or garbage can lid (for campfires where permitted), matches
- Tent

Basics for the daypack
Every daypack packed for desert hiking should include a basic list of items:
- Map (7.5 minute USGS topographic maps for specific area), compass
- Sunglasses (and a spare pair), sunscreen, hat
- Hat (brimmed, light-colored to reflect the sun)
- Sturdy boots with insoles
- Water (at least 2-4 liters minimum) with electrolyte replacement powder and energy food/snacks/lunch
- Clothing (layers)
- Matches in a waterproof container or plastic baggie
- Flashlight
- First-aid kit with the following basic items:
  - Waterproof tape (good for wrapping heels and toes to prevent blisters)
  - Moleskin (good for wrapping heels and toes to prevent blisters)
  - Neosporin (anti-bacterial ointment)
  - Alcohol pads
  - Blistex (or other anti-chapping ointment)
  - Small bottle of bug repellent
  - Tweezers (for removing cactus spines)
  - Needle-nose pliers (for removing cholla spines)
  - Roll of gauze/gauze pads; ace bandage (for sprains)
  - Band-aids
  - Whistle
  - Aspirin (or acetaminophen for high altitude–not as apt to cause stomach upset)
  - Antacid

Geologic Time Scale

ERA	PERIOD	EPOCH	YEARS
Cenozoic (Age of Mammals)	Quaternary	Holocene	
		————————— 10,000	
		Pleistocene	
		————————————— 2-3 million	
	Tertiary	Pliocene	
		————————— 12 million	
		Miocene	
		————————— 26 million	
		Oligocene	
		————————— 37-38 million	
		Eocene	
		————————— 53-54 million	
		Paleocene	
		————————————— 65 million	
Mesozoic (Age of Reptiles)	Cretaceous	————————————— 136 million	
	Jurassic		
		————————————— 190-195 million	
	Triassic		
		————————————— 225 million	
Paleozoic (Age of Fishes)	Permian	————————————— 280 million	
	Pennsylvanian		
		————————————— 320 million	
	Mississippian		
		————————————— 345 million	
	Devonian		
		————————————— 395 million	
	Silurian		
		————————————— 430-440 million	
	Ordovician		
		————————————— 500 million	
	Cambrian		
		————————————— 570 million	
Precambrian			
	Origin of the Earth		4.6 billion

DESERT TRAVEL TIPS

BY ANDY ZDON FROM THE SPOTTED DOG PRESS GUIDE BOOK
DESERT SUMMITS: A CLIMBING AND HIKING GUIDE TO
CALIFORNIA AND SOUTHERN NEVADA

Most of the desert trails in this book are located in remote, unpopulated areas and are out of cell phone range. Before traveling in the desert make sure someone knows your travel plans and destinations, when you plan to return. Carry plenty of water (in at least two separate containers), extra food and supplies, good maps, tool kit, a good spare and suitable tire jack.

MAPS

Do not depend on the maps in this book! They are for general reference only and do not include the details found in a good road or USGS topo map. Carry a complete set of maps for each destination and know how to read them.

VEHICLE MAINTENANCE

At a minimum, your vehicle is in good running condition with a set of tools, a working jack and an inflated spare tire. A can of puncture seal can work wonders in a pinch.

Check the belts, fans and cooling system. The radiator should have the correct amount of coolant. We always carry an extra bottle of coolant. Tires should have plenty of tread remaining and should be properly inflated. Once on the way to the remote Saline Valley hot springs, we got a flat tire. The Hi-Lift Jack that looked so cool on the back bumper didn't work on a Japanese make vehicle, so we resorted to using the undersized jack. Once the tire was changed, everyone questioned whether or not we should return to civilization instead of going on to the springs. "What are the odds of getting a second flat tire?" I asked. We continued on and just short of the springs a second tire went flat. What now? I had a can of puncture seal which held the tire long enough to make it back to the town of Big Pine just before midnight.

WATER AND SUPPLIES

Carry extra water, food, matches, twine or rope, sunscreen, camping gear, (blankets or sleeping bag if going for the day).

If the car breaks down or gets trapped in deep sand: Keep calm and stay with your car! The car will provide shade and shelter and can be seen more easily from the ground and air than a person wandering through creosote and scrub. Inventory your supplies and conserve your strength. Use your headlights at night and honk that horn. As scary as it seems, someone will eventually come along. Sadly, people die all the time wandering away from their broken down cars in the desert. A few years ago, a woman's car broke down in Goler Wash (Death Valley), a remote yet well-traveled road, for a desert road. Instead of staying with the vehicle she tried to walk out and died of dehydration and heat stroke.

We once traveled the "Harry Wade Escape Route" in a low-slung Volkswagen Scirocco, despite the fact that several signs warned at the onset that the road was not maintained and very remote. The car got caught in deep sand. We tried to dig it out, then considered our options, when from the opposite direction, came a four-wheel drive with a Swiss professor and his family here on sabbatical. He was elated to make a desert rescue using his new vehicle's winch.

Avoid parking or traveling in dry washes and gullies. Storms miles away from your location often fill the gullies and washes miles downstream. Leave the car and head for high ground in an emergency. Many lives and a few townsites have been lost over the past fifty years in western deserts because of unpredictable flash floods.

TEMPERATURE

Deserts can have an enormous temperature range within a twenty-four hour period. Under certain conditions, a few hours may be the difference between a freezing dawn and a 100-degree day in a shadeless canyon exposed to the direct rays of the sun. Long-sleeved, wind proof garments should be carried, and may be needed to protect the climber from the cold, wind, or direct rays of the sun. Take short but frequent snack breaks every forty-five minutes to an hour of hiking, and wear a light-colored broad-brimmed hat. During late spring, summer, and early fall (in the lower elevations) hike when the trails and canyons are shaded, usually from dawn to late morning or from late afternoon to dusk. Avoid hiking in the sun, and in particular, avoid hiking uphill during the hottest part of the day. When we climbed Avawatz Peak in the Mojave Desert (during early summer), we started hiking around four in the morning, making for some very pleasant hiking. By the time we reached the car shortly before noon, the temperature had risen to over 100 degrees. If there is water to spare, dousing the top of one's head every forty-five minutes can be very refreshing on a hot day.

Heat-related Illness

Heat exhaustion is a serious heat-related illness that occurs when the body rate of heat gain is greater than the rate of heat loss. The best way to avoid heat exhaustion is to drink adequate water with electrolyte additives. Several factors can cause heat exhaustion, dehydration and over exertion when it's hot are the two biggest causes. Symptoms include physical weakness, dizziness, nausea, vomiting, minimal or no urination and headache. When symptoms are identified, the victim should move (or be moved) out of direct sunlight, sit or lie down (preferably with feet elevated somewhat), and slowly drink a fluid such as water with electrolyte replacements. Future movement should be limited until the body's fluids are restored.

Heat stroke occurs when the body's internal temperature rises above 105 degrees, and results in death if not treated immediately. Hikers or mountaineers who are not used to hot temperatures like those found in the desert, may suffer from "exertional heat stroke" if they prolong their activity. Their initial symptoms will include pale, damp, cool skin even when their internal temperature has reached dangerous levels, followed by confusion, irrational, even aggressive behavior and physical collapse. Others will exhibit symptoms of classic heat stroke in which their skin will be hot and dry to the touch. In both cases, the goal of treatment is to reduce the body temperature quickly. The victim should be placed in the shade, tight clothing removed or loosened, and cooled by swabbing with water-soaked cloths or bandanas, and fanning. If the victim is conscious, have them drink water in sips. The victim must be carried out and hospitalized.

HYPOTHERMIA

During the winter, or at higher elevations, during any time of the year, hypothermia can be one of the principal hazards to the desert climber. Hypothermia occurs when the body experiences heat loss causing the body's core temperature to drop, impairing brain and muscular functions. The most common way for the desert climber to become hypothermic is by not dressing warmly enough to insulate the body from the cold environment. Initial symptoms may include feeling very cold, numbness of skin, and minor muscular impairment. As the body temperature drops, the muscles become increasingly uncoordinated, there is mild confusion, slowness of pace, apathy or amnesia. If not treated immediately, it can progress to unconsciousness and eventually death.

Preventing hypothermia requires warm dry clothing, food and water. Again, drinking water and snacking on foods high in carbohydrates at frequent intervals will provide energy supplies for physical activity and production of body heat. Most important, dress in layers. Wool and polyester are the best insulators. A layer of polypropylene long underwear, tops and bottoms, followed by wool or synthetic sweater and pants, topped off with a waterproof, breathable layer of nylon, jackets and pants that can double as rain and wind protection. The final critical item is a wool or polyester weave hat since most heat loss occurs from the head. Include on the list, a warm pair of gloves and socks. If a person comes down with hypothermia, removing wet clothes and warming them with another human body can be a lifesaver. If a sleeping bag is handy, climbing into the sleeping bag with them can help restore their body temperature.

DEHYDRATION

Low humidity, high temperatures, and brisk winds draw water from a person at a rate that seems impossible to climbers not familiar with the desert's arid environment. Streams seldom exist; desert water holes are far apart and easily missed by those not versed with the desert landscape. A climber who boasts that he never carries a water bottle will find that he may need as much as a gallon of water under certain circumstances. Dehydration and heat-related illnesses account for most of the injuries and rescues throughout the year in desert terrain. Muscle cramps in the legs or the abdomen can result from the loss of water and electrolytes. Certainly, no attempt to climb a mountain should be made with less than two quarts of water or other liquids combined with an electrolyte replacement supplement. With temperatures exceeding 100 degrees in canyon floors, and humidity dropping below 10%, twenty-four hours without water can be fatal to an inexperienced hiker. The author commonly carries up to four liters of water for a full day's outing on a warm day.

The flip side of dehydration is "hyponatremia" or water intoxication. Hyponatremia occurs when a person drinks an excessive amount of water without replacing lost electrolytes either by not eating or not including an electrolyte replacement supplement in their water. Initial symptoms are similar to those of heat exhaustion—physical weakness, dizziness, nausea with frequent urination, and eventually seizures, collapse, and unconsciousness.

Depending on desert watering holes can be a very risky business and is thoroughly not recommended in this guidebook. O.E. Meinzer, a U.S.G.S. hydrologist who studied springs in the California desert once wrote:

"The desert has a peculiar fascination. Its solitude and silence are soothing to man...if he comes at the end of a long day, with a tired and thirsty team of horses, to an isolated watering place that has gone dry, or if he loses his bearings and the panorama assumes a strange and bewildering aspect...his feelings toward the desert will undergo a sudden change."

Not only will your attitude toward the desert change, but without water, you will have far greater issues to worry about than attitude adjustments.

UNFRIENDLY VEGETATION

Many desert plants, that provide important habitat for desert wildlife, while delightful to view and photograph, are unfriendly or even injurious on contact. Although there are none of the "man-eating plants" seen in many 1950's era science fictions, a 10-foot fall into an agave can be just as deadly. The cacti and yuccas are well-known hazards. The cholla, which some claim can jump at a passer-by, earning the nickname "jumping cholla," has spines that break freely and defy attempts to pull them from the flesh unless tweezers or even needle-nose pliers are available. The agave has sword-like leaves that can fatally impale a falling rock climber. The catclaw can tear the shirt (and skin) right off your back. However, just because the complacent hiker may occasionally tangle with these plants, don't look harshly upon them. Desert flora are an integral part of nature's landscape.

DESERT CREATURES

The desert is home to many native species of animals, birds, insects and lizards, all of which have carved out a balanced and delicate niche in this arid environment of extreme heat and cold. Many are nocturnal, protected by the shade of burrow or nest during the day, and out and about doing their business at night. It is a wonderful and fascinating world to observe from a distance. This is their home, and we are only visitors, so they deserve our respect. They also don't expect us to come crashing around the corner, so a chance encounter with a surprised creature is always a possibility. Several times, the author has heard the rattle of a snake's tail before ever seeing the snake curled up beneath the cool shade of a rocky crevice in a gully. The sound is always enough to send one flying out of harm's way.

Watch where you step and put your hands. The desert is home to scorpions, centipedes, cone-nosed bloodsuckers (aka kissing bugs), rattlesnakes, bees, wasps, hornets, tarantulas, skunks, stinkbugs, biting gnats, ticks, and non-native grazing animals like skitish and unpredictable range cattle. Add the Africanized Honey Bee to this list. This non-native insect that is virtually indistinguishable from normal honey bees, and has already been identified in several areas covered by this guide. This bee doesn't simply sting when it's disturbed. It invites thousands of its friends in on the fun, and the result can be fatal. It is virtually impossible to outrun these fellows. On my trips to the desert, I have rarely seen bees. If you do see them, be careful as it is very possible they may be the Africanized Honey Bee. Step gingerly over downed logs, as they are a favorite hive location.

One way to avoid many of the inspects and spiders described above is to shake out your shoes and clothes before putting them on. Shoes removed at night are a favorite warm spot for insects and spiders to nest. The author recalls putting on his hiking boots at camp only to feel a crunch inside his shoe, the result of the squashing of a poor beetle that had taken shelter in that leather abode.

Scorpions are often found under rocks, downed wood, and in cracks and on ledges of rock piles. Two spiders to watch out for are the black widow and the brown recluse. Black widows are particularly common around old desert shacks, old cans, and wood piles. Rattlesnakes are prevalent throughout the desert southwest, and a run-in with one of these creatures can be a serious affair. Rattlesnakes will not chase anything they can't swallow and will leave you alone unless they feel threatened.

Centipedes, tarantulas, cone-nosed bloodsuckers, biting ants, wasps, and bees are common desert dwellers and can inflict a painful, but non-dangerous bite. Simply wash the bite with an alcohol pad (soap and water if in camp), treat with an antiseptic, and take an aspirin for the pain which will subside after a few hours.

Hantavirus is a concern wherever there are mice. This airborne virus, carried by the deer mouse, is present in its urine and feces. When this material is disturbed, the infected particles can become airborne and inhaled by the unsuspecting individual. To minimize the possibility of getting this frequently fatal virus, avoid contact with rodents and rodent burrows, dilapidated buildings (such as old desert shacks) that show evidence of rodent activity, don't sleep on bare ground, keep food in rodent-proof containers, use only bottled or disinfected water, and don't feed or play with mice.

After reading this section you may think, "Sounds too dangerous for me." Hiking in the desert is much safer than your daily commute to work. For more educated reading on the subject, pick up a copy of the excellent source book POISONOUS DWELLERS OF THE DESERT by Trevor Hare.

LIGHTNING

Lightning in the desert is most commonly a threat during the summer thunderstorm season. The high ranges are especially vulnerable to severe lightning storms, and it is the high desert ranges that are most likely climbed during the summer months, after the snow melts. If caught in a lightning storm, there are a few places you definitely do not want to be: under an exposed tree or worse yet, at a summit microwave or repeater installation; on any exposed high ridge; or out in the open anywhere regardless of elevation. Don't wait for the hair on your arms to start standing on end (due to the build of atmospheric charge) to minimize your exposure.

ABANDONED MINES

One of the fascinating aspects of climbing in the desert is that inevitably, old, abandoned mines, and outbuildings, that provoke curiosity and exploration, will be encountered. Investigating the areas around these mines can be as interesting as the hike. However, there are a few potential hazards associated with abandoned mines. A fall down an unmarked shaft is likely to be lethal. Miners have been known to leave behind explosives, old dynamite sticks, blasting caps and powder, most likely unstable, inside and outside mines. If you happen upon such a cache, leave them alone and report their presence to the local land management agency.

Even more hazards await the curious in tunnels and other underground workings: blind shafts hidden beneath a seemingly innocent puddle of surface water, cave-ins, and bad air (air containing poisonous gasses, or more likely, insufficient oxygen) are some of the most common. Many an old mine was abandoned because of fire. Timbers can smolder for years until the oxygen in the tunnel is gone. Poor ventilation may cause an oxygen deficient atmosphere to last for decades, and in places oxygen content in the air may be low enough to cause unconsciousness before the explorer knows what happened. Other underground hazards include cave-ins, decayed timbers that can fall on the climber, or ladders with weak rungs. The best advice is to stay out of underground mine workings.

Confusing Landmarks

To the novice, desert mountain ranges look pretty similar. The steep barren canyons have few distinguishing characteristics for the person who is unaccustomed to them, or can't identify landmarks. All instructions for route-finding should be applied here, much more so than in alpine mountains. Before heading off into the remote desert, a knowledge of compass-work and navigation is recommended. Learn to identify landmarks on the way–an odd-shaped rock formation; a lone Joshua tree on an otherwise treeless terrain . . . these can all help locate yourself. Look behind you on your way up and pinpoint a landmark, perhaps where the car is parked so you can identify the route on the way down.

A note about following those small piles of rocks called "cairns" or "ducks." Frequently, these small piles of rock mark the route to a desert summit. Other times, they may denote the route to someone's mining claim, or may be a claim marker themselves (the standard wood posts in the desert weren't too popular in the old days considering the lack of trees). They may even have been placed by someone

Along the Excelsior Mine Road. PHOTO: WYNNE BENTI

with the same summit goal but who was hopelessly lost and didn't realize it. Blindly following these piles of rocks puts you in the position of trusting the orienteering of others, and possibly putting your life in the hands of someone you don't know. It is best to learn to use the compass, learn to read the maps and terrain, and choose your own route.

UNSTABLE TERRAIN

Rain falls sparsely in the desert. Rocks and boulders that appear to be securely embedded in slopes often break loose and roll when touched. Smaller rocks that look stable become loose, dumping the climber to the ground (or even into a cactus). With large parties, these rolling rocks are as dangerous as the cannonading of rocks on glacial climbs. When desert granite decomposes on its surface, the resulting particles often remain in place, providing a ball-bearing effect, tripping up the unsuspecting hiker. Other rock fragments that appear to be firmly in place break loose when stepped upon, again with the same result.

DESERT ROADS

Traveling along the desert back roads leading to many of the peaks described in this book can be more dangerous than the climbs themselves. Always let someone know your plans. Be sure to contact local land management agencies before your trip to check on conditions. Approach roads are often mere tracks across desert washes, perhaps a long-abandoned route to a forgotten mine site. High centers are hazardous to cars. Sand pockets will trap the inexperienced (and often experienced) driver, and a drop of one foot into one of these sand traps may take hours of digging to escape. Memories of trying to unstick a gutless, old economy car, from the deep sand of Yuma Wash in southwestern Arizona, in the middle of the night comes to mind. Thankfully the weather was fine and the clear moonless night was pleasant, even beautiful. The same situation at a hotter time could have been a serious predicament.

If you become stuck or your car breaks down, don't attempt to walk away from your vehicle, particularly if its hot and the walk is many miles. The people who know about your trip will know where to look for you assuming no one else happens by to lend a hand. It is much easier for a search party to find a car than a solitary hiker. Once, while on a college field trip in Death Valley, our van happened to get a flat tire along a hot, dry, and seemingly unpopulated expanse of dirt road. We were dismayed to find that a lug wrench and jack-stand were not included with our van, and we had no way of changing the tire. Instead of taking on the hot afternoon sun and hiking out, the group decided to stay put. We had our camping gear, and plenty of food and water. To our surprise, within a few hours, a van load of tourists happened by and allowed us the use of their equipment. The timing of their arrival was perfect for them too. They discovered they also had a tire going flat!

Sudden flash floods can cut across these "roads." If storm clouds are present, better to let a summit go unclimbed than attempt a drive up or crossing a desert dry wash. That dry wash can become a raging torrent, rivaling a large mountain river, in a very brief period of time. If venturing more than a few miles beyond frequently traveled roads, a party should consist of not less than two cars, with much more gas and water than you expect to use. When venturing onto the desert back roads, check the condition of your vehicle first. Start with a full gas tank, check the fluid levels, tire pressure and wear, and the condition of your hoses. The Bureau of Land Management recommends that the following equipment be carried in your car: a basic tool kit with a full socket set, pliers, wrenches, screwdrivers and the like; spark plug socket; wire cutters; vice grips; channel locks; allen wrenches; hammer, knife, spare tire and jack; a tow strap; first aid kit; duct tape (one of the world's great inventions); shop manual for your car; air pressure gauge and tire inflater; shovel; fire extinguisher; flashlight and batteries; jumper cables; and three gallons of water per person plus five gallons of water per vehicle.

Always practice minimum impact camping. The ultimate goal of everyone who makes a trip to the desert should be to come and go without leaving a trace of their visit. Stay on established roads and obey all land management agency signs concerning road access. It really is important to stay on established roads and not to cut new ones through the desert scrub. Because the desert doesn't get much rain, it can take decades for destroyed desert plants to get enough water to grow again. A sport utility vehicle (SUV) that leaves an established road just once, does devastating damage that can last for a century. During spring, native and migratory birds build their nests in desert shrubs. The author has seen nests crushed by SUV wheels that left an established road because the driver didn't know how to drive through a stretch of sand or was too lazy to get out of the vehicle and do a little road work to make the established route passable. If everyone who owns an SUV, ATV or any kind of OHV, were to drive like they do in the TV commercials (GONZO off established roads), the desert would be a gutted, irreparable mess. Years of neglect and abuse have already done extensive damage. The Bureau of Land Management has set aside desert areas specifically designated for Off-Highway Vehicle use.

A few other pointers. When hiking on established trails (or even faint climbers' paths) stay on them. Taking shortcuts, known as "cutting switchbacks" will erode the trail. Pack out what you pack in (carry out all garbage). Always dig a hole at least eight inches deep to bury your human waste. Pack out toilet paper in a ziplock bag or bury it. If you need to burn it, do it carefully, and make sure the fire is dead out! Entire forests have been burned to the ground by this practice, and a desert range fire is a difficult fire to fight. Always camp at least 100 feet from any water source be it a rare desert stream or spring. Remember: "Leave no trace."

Now that we've covered all of these potentially deadly hazards, you may ask, so why go?

As our friend, Walt Wheelock, once said:

"The freedoms from man's trials and tribulations,

the warm dry air and peacefulness of a desert camp,

when the rest of the world's mountains are snowed in,

are the days that a guidebook can point toward,

but are only found by going to these regions."

Walt Wheelock

BIBLIOGRAPHIC SOURCES
& REFERENCE READING

Background to Historic and Prehistoric Resources of the East Mojave Desert Region by Dennis Casebier. BLM, Riverside, 1976. Information on the Mojave Wagon Road, excellent bibliography.

The California Deserts by Edmund C. Jaeger. Stanford University Press, Stanford, rev. 1955. A complete work on these deserts including geology, plants, animals, etc.

Death Valley to Yosemite: Frontier Mining Camps and Ghost Towns by *L. Burr Belden and Mary DeDecker,* Spotted Dog Press, Bishop, CA, 2000. Guide to ghost towns and camps east of the Sierra Nevada.

Desert Summits: A Climbing and Hiking Guide to California and Southern Nevada by Andy Zdon. Spotted Dog Press, Bishop, CA, 2000. Most extensive guide to California desert peaks ever written.

The Enduring Desert by E.I. Edwards. Ward Ritchie Press, Los Angeles, 1969. A descriptive bibliography. Extensive, accurate and beautifully printed.

Forgotten Army Posts of the Mojave by L. Burr Belden. In Westerners Brand Book XI, Los Angeles, 1964.

Golden Mirages by Philip Bailey. Macmillian Co., New York, 1940. A classic in the realm of lost treasure tales.

Guidebook to the Mojave Desert of California by Russ Leadabrand. Ward Ritchie Press, Los Angeles, 1966.

Heritage o' the Valley, San Bernardino: First Century by Helen and George Beattie. San Pasquel Press, Pasadena, 1939.

Jack Mitchell, Caveman by BaileyTimherlakePailey. Torrance, 1964. Mitchell's own story of the Caverns.

Mojave Road Guide by Dennis Casebier and the Friends of the Mojave Road. Tales of the Mojave Road Publishing Company, Norco, California 1986

Nevada, An Annotated Bibliography by Stanley Pahar. Nevada Publications, Las Vegas, 1980. Invaluable to researchers.

Nevada's Turbulant Yesteryear by Con Ashbaugh. Westernlore Press, Los Angeles, 1963. A study in ghost towns.

Out From Las Vegas: Adventures A Day Away by Florine Lawlor. Spotted Dog Press, Bishop, CA, 2002. Trips into the backcountry near Las Vegas.

Railroads of Nevada and Eastern California. Vol 2 by David Myrick. Howell North Books, Berkeley, 1963. Covers many of the small mining roads as well as the main lines.

Record of Travels in Arizona and California 1775-1776 by Father Francisco Garces, John Galvin, editor. John HowellBooks, San Francisco 1965.

Reports of Exploration for a Railway Route Near the Thirty-fifth Parallel from the Mississippi River to the Pacific Ocean, Vol. 3 by A.W.Whipple., Senate Ex.Doc No. 78, 1856.

The Rocks Begin to Speak by Martineau Lavan. KC Publications, Las Vegas, 1973. An attempt to translate petroglyphs.

Rocky Trails of the Past by Charles Labbe. Self-published, Las Vegas, 1960. Stories of mining towns in Nevada and Southern California.

Southern California Atlas and Gazetteer published by DeLorme Publishing Co., Freeport, Maine, 1986.

Trails Through the Golden West by Robert Frothingham. Robert McBride and Co., 1932. References to Death Valley

INDEX

SPOTTED DOG PRESS

WWW.SPOTTEDDOGPRESS.COM ORDER FORM

Mail to:
Spotted Dog Press
P.O. Box 1721
Bishop CA 93515
800-417-2790
FAX 760-872-1319

Name:		
Address:		
City	State	Zip Code
Daytime Phone:		
Credit card #:		Exp. Date:
Signature		

Title	Price	Quantity	Total
High & Wild Galen Rowell *Hard Cover* 224 full color pages. Considered to be Galen Rowell's best mountain writing and photography. 23 new stories. A beautiful work. Hard cover with dust jacket.	**$34.95**		
Close Ups of the High Sierra II Norman Clyde 176 pages. NEW EDITION 2004. A new edition of Norman Clyde's writings.	**14.95**		
Climbing Mt. Whitney Benti & Wheelock 80 pages. Information on permits, route descriptions, how to hike Whitney as a dayhike, backpack, moonlight hike or rock climb. Everything you need to know to get to the top of the highest peak in the contiguous U.S.	**8.95**		
Death Valley to Yosemite: Frontier Mining Camps and Ghost Towns Belden & DeDecker 192 pages. The most complete work available today on the mining camps from the Mojave Desert to the High Sierra. Beautifully written by two exceptional authors with detailed maps showing locations.	**14.95**		
Desert Summits: A Climbing & Hiking Guide to California and Southern Nevada Andy Zdon 418 pages. Definitive guide to the highpoints of California's and Southern Nevada's desert ranges from the Great Basin to the Mexican border.	**19.95**		
Favorite Dog Hikes in and Around Los Angeles Benti 160 pages. The best-selling trail guide to the dog trails of Los Angeles. With a pattern for making dog hiking boots.	**12.95**		
Grand Canyon Treks Harvey Butchart 288 pages. Butchart walked, air mattressed and climbed more than 12,000 miles in the Grand Canyon backcountry and is considered the leading authority.	**16.95**		
Out From Las Vegas Florine Lawlor 288 pages. Guide to more than sixty adventures within a day's drive of Las Vegas by newspaper and travel reporter, Las Vegas native, Florine Lawlor.	**16.95**		
Born Free and Equal Ansel Adams *Hard Cover* 128 pages. New edition written and photographed by Adams from 1943-1944 at Manzanar War Relocation Center. His most important social work.	**45.00**		
The Secret Sierra David Gilligan 288 pages. Explore the hidden world of the Sierra Nevada's alpine zone through the eyes of a naturalist.	**18.95**		
	Subtotal		
	UPS Shipping $4.00 all orders!		
CA residents please add 7.25% sales tax	**7.25% CA Sales Tax**		
Make check or money order payable to: Spotted Dog Press, P.O. Box 1721, Bishop, CA 93515-1721	**Total**		